Names and places have been altered to protect the privacy of those involved.

I Died a Little Every Night

ANGEL COSTELLO

authorHOUSE®

AuthorHouse™
1663 Liberty Drive
Bloomington, IN 47403
www.authorhouse.com
Phone: 1-800-839-8640

First published by AuthorHouse   4/25/2011

ISBN: 978-1-4567-6183-7 (e)
ISBN: 978-1-4567-6184-4 (hc)
ISBN: 978-1-4567-6186-8 (sc)

Library of Congress Control Number: 2011906300

Printed in the United States of America

Thank you to everyone that helped me to get to where I am right now.

To all the Angels that the Lord gave to me Diamond, Dave and Meghan.

Contents

ANGEL 1974

My Special Butterfly

I recall as a little girl just a few
years back
My thinking place was a set of old
railroad tracks
I sat and dream for hours among the
trees and beautiful wild flowers
I was lonely in those days and it made
the time go by
When I could find a butterfly
They are the most beautiful things a human can see
I'd make believe that they were my friends
and they really liked me
There would be days that went by that my only friend
would be a butterfly
In my wildest dreams I never imagined
I'd be blessed with such a beautiful charm
As I look over and the nurse is laying you on my arm
And remember this Angel dear
Until the day you die
You'll always be my special butterfly

By: Lillian

Introduction

Let this story take you on a young girl's decade long journey of abuse at the hands of her step-father Leon.

From the ages of six to sixteen, Angel endured multiple forms of physical, sexual and emotional abuse that led her in to a drug fueled life of sex and rebellion.

From a family with a long history of violence and abuse; Angel grew from a child of stolen innocence into a young woman pregnant with the seed of her abuser. It seemed the cycle of abuse would never end and the emotional toll would last a lifetime.

Never be bullied into silence. Never allow yourself to be made a victim. Accept no one's definition of your life; define yourself.

-Harvey Fierstein

"Why Am I Here"

As you looked around Caribou, Maine all you can see for miles are fields. The town itself had only one small grocery store and a small school of one hundred and six students. It is here that two teenage kids foolishly fell in love. While freely spirited on the outside, they were trapped on the inside.

Lillian, whom everyone called Lil, was the youngest of five; two boys and three girls. They lived in what some people would call a shack- only one bedroom and an outside bathroom. There was absolutely no money to speak of. Her father received a small disability check and her mother stayed home.

Lil's mother was a woman who wore her heart on her sleeve for anyone's taking. She was abused physically and mentally by her husband and second to oldest son. She never dared say no and would give anyone what they wanted. She gave birth to Lil at the age of fifty-three. Some people would say that was the reason why Lil learned slower than other children in school and in life.

Lil's father was small and had such bad arthritis his hands crumpled toward him. People around town would ask how someone could be so small and brittle yet still be so powerful that he caused so much pain towards everyone around him.

Lil's mother died when Lil was only eighteen. Rumors went around that being beat so many times in the head was the cause of her mother's death from a brain tumor. Her father lived for three more years before dying of natural causes. Her oldest brother went off to the army and left the next son to take care of the family and be the man of the house. Unfortunately he grew up to be much like his father, and the mental and physical abuse toward the girls continued. Lil was very young when her older brother started to molest her and one of her sisters. This was the start of many family secrets that were hidden in the closet.

Bradley was the oldest of seven children. His family also had no money and lived in a run down home. However he had something to be grateful for because there wasn't any abuse in his home. Bradley, whom everyone called Brad, was loved by his parents. His father had a heart of gold; his only problem was alcoholism. This may have been part of the reason Brad started drinking at the age of fifteen. His mother who was the disciplinarian also had a good heart and would help anyone who was in need. When she died of natural causes, the whole family counted on Brad to be the rock. He took care of them right up until the day his father died eighteen years later of a heart attack.

Lil and Brad started going steady at the age of fifteen. It wasn't long after that they announced their love for one another in a field surrounded by wild flowers. At the age of seventeen, they moved out of their run down homes and moved in with each other. Things went good for a few years, and then Brad started to cheat on Lil. It didn't take long for her to develop low self-esteem and think it was something she was doing wrong that made him cheat. She forgave him over and over again, and they married when they were only nineteen. Not long after the wedding Lil found out that she was pregnant but Brad continued to cheat on her not only with strangers but with friends and relatives. Now, looking back Brad will tell anyone who asks that Lil was better looking than any of those women that he had slept with.

On April 11, 1973, Lil gave birth to a healthy, beautiful baby girl. They decided to name her Angel Mae. Lil knew that she would again have to try to forgive and forget Brad's cheating and stay for the sake of Angel. She managed to hang on for three more years. Three more years of fighting, cheating and forgiving. By then Lil had had enough and filed for divorce. Yet once again she forgave him and they remarried. Brad thought he would be able to change but not long after they remarried she heard him on the phone with another woman. A year later they divorced again.

This is where Angel's story begins.

First Memories

AGE 5

From then on Angel rarely heard from her dad, he had moved to Connecticut with the woman Lil heard him cheating with on the phone. Lil thought that if he lived only three hours away from her, he would see Angel every other weekend or so. It never even started out as every other weekend or so. At first, it started out as every other month, then every Christmas and on her birthday. Lil tried to bite her tongue when she explained to Angel why her dad wasn't coming to see her; she would make excuses after excuse for him. How could she tell a five year old the truth - that her father was a selfish bastard and thought only of himself, that his little Angel was no longer his princess and his one and only reason for living, that now he had a whole new family, and that his first family will now be pushed under the rug.

Angel had only a few memories of events before the age of six. The first memory of childhood was the day her father, leaned down and gave her a kiss on the forehead, said bye and walked out the door. On that day he left her mother and her for good. Angel was only four and a half. That kiss was the last time she was kissed by a man who truly loved her. After that her mother would walk around the house with a blank stare doing laundry, dishes, mopping - all the while crying.

Lil decided to pack up her and Angel's things and move to Lincoln, New Hampshire when Angel was five. Lincoln was a lot like Caribou - meaning there were houses where fields may have been, but the people were the same. Everyone knew everyone, and they talked like they were friends when face-to-face. But, once you turned the other way you were faced with the same friends telling you about how so and so is sleeping with her friend's husband, or how she is so neglectful towards her children they should be taken away. Lil would listen but not talk about her own life; she was taught that what happened in your home stayed in your home.

Angel and her mother lived on Homestead Street, in an apartment that had only one bedroom that they shared. Their building was surrounded on all sides by more buildings that all looked alike. They were all large and grey with red shutters. The cars had only one way in and one way out. In the middle of the buildings was a basketball court. This is where most of the kids played basketball and jumped rope. Even the small children could tell it was a rundown neighborhood.

Angel started going to school at Woodster Heights Elementary. It was around a mile from where they lived. Lil made sure she moved into a place within walking distance from town and the school, since many mornings went by when the car wouldn't start. They shivered in the cold while walking to school, but Angel remembers those mornings filled with fun and adventure. Lil would always make the walk into a story. When Angel walked into school there would be kids waiting to hear the story her mother had just told her.

Everyday Angel couldn't wait to go to school. Her favorite teacher was her first grade teacher, Ms. Little. Her sense of fashion is what drew Angel to her first. She didn't wear the same turtleneck and sweaters that all the rest of the teachers wore. She'd wear plaid mini skirts with thigh high boots and her hair was the biggest Afro Angel had ever seen. She was the sort of teacher that you could tell anything to. On numerous occasions when Angel had a loose tooth, Ms. Little would get a soft tissue and tell Angel to close her eyes. With a little turn and a soft touch the tooth would come out into the tissue. Angel didn't have many friends at school, and she believed it had a lot to do with how much she respected and helped Ms. Little. She would stay after school just to help her clean the chalkboards or sharpen pencils for the next day. Kids often called her a teacher's pet.

In Angel's neighborhood there were many families, and at home Angel had lots of friends. There was one family that had four children and another on the way, but they stayed in their home most of the time. Then there was the family that had three children: Selina, William and Saundra. In the apartment building behind Angel's was another family with four children: Victoria, Steven, Mona and Ricky. Angel was the only one that didn't have any siblings, so all the other children became like her sisters and brothers.   Lillian's sister, Anne, also lived in the neighborhood. She had two sons, Patrick and Henry. They were teenagers and they were wild. They started a gang made up of six boys that they called the "six-pack", and they'd always raise hell. Lil said it was strange that Patrick and Henry were so bad seeing as how Anne was a Sunday school teacher.

After school all the kids would run home and play carnival. They picked up every piece of wood, cloth and metal around them and used it for games and rides. On a good day they would find what they called the treasure, which was a grocery cart from the store down the road.

While Angel played for hours, Lil hunted for another apartment. Lil wanted one that had two bedrooms. One became available that was right beside her sister Anne's apartment. The building was still located in the same courtyard but the apartment itself was much bigger than their first one. But with more room, came more problems. Angel would be afraid to open the drawers knowing that there would be cockroaches inside. The wallpaper was peeling, and the faucets would spray out water all over the place.

Lil would go over to Anne's apartment everyday, they talked non-stop. Lil also became friends with almost everyone she came into contact with, because they all had similar lives.

It was a comfortable place to live. No one got picked on for not wearing nice clothes or for not having any money. The kids got together during the day, and at night, when all the kids were supposed to be in bed, the grown ups gathered.

All the parents would have a party of their own outside. On occasion, if you looked up at the windows you would notice a small child's face watching in amazement. Everyone would be either, drinking, smoking pot or sometimes worse. At times, when too much alcohol was consumed, friends would start fights - real throw downs. There would be blood and sometimes a rush to the hospital.

Between the six-pack and the grown ups, the cops got to know Homestead Street really well. Usually they would make at least one appearance a night to calm things down. Everyone always made up the very next day if they were one of the ones that were fighting.

When Brad and Lil divorced, they went to court over child support. Brad pleaded with the court saying he had no money. He was ordered to pay only ten dollars a month. That may have seemed like a lot years ago, but even then ten dollars couldn't get you a decent meal. Even so the money stopped coming after only three months. Sometimes Lil would get very upset with the way they were living. She would throw her hands up, start crying and yell "I'm calling your father".

Everyone knew Brad had more money than he claimed he did. Angel went to his house for one week the summer after they moved, and even at that young age knew that things were better for him. There was always food in the cupboards and refrigerator even though Brad often had two or more people living with him and his new wife Denise. Everyone always had nice clothes to wear and a good car to drive.

Angel loved seeing her Dad during that time but never got along with Denise. Angel didn't really know what jealousy was until she met Denise. Every time Angel would sit near her dad, Denise would squeeze in between them, as if this precious little girl was going to steal her new husband away from her. Although she felt like she was his baby girl, his princess, Angel was only able to sit on his lap twice as a child when Denise was around.

When it was time for Angel to go home after visits, Denise would make it a very short goodbye. It was funny how with every father - daughter hug or kiss, Denise developed a headache or stomach ache, which was so bad, it urged her Dad to leave and bring her home real fast.

It was like when she left her dad's house she didn't exist to him until the next summer. He would never send any money for them, although there was one Christmas and one birthday where after opening the one or two presents he brought he handed Angel a card behind his back with a hundred dollar bill in it. Angel begged to go to her favorite store - Kmart - where she bought her mom a new shirt and necklace and new socks and underwear for herself.

Going home Angel had to go back to reality. Lil was a seamstress making minimum wage. They never had any food in the cupboards or refrigerator, and they made a monthly stroll down to the Salvation Army to get a new outfit that would cost around a dollar or two. No one knew where the outfit came from thanks to her mom sewing a piece of ribbon here or a bow there so she fit right in with the other kids at school.

Lil never seemed happy those days. Everyone had someone to love except for her. She would date men, but when she would try to get serious with them, it would always end because of Angel. She wanted a guy to love Angel; one who didn't drink, smoke, cheat or lie. There were very little of those men around the neighborhood. Even the kids of all her friends had found love real young, usually with someone from the neighborhood. Most of the teenagers would hang outside and cuddle. Angel would sit and watch her mom smile when they kissed or hugged. It was as if she was finding happiness among their smiles.

Kisses

AGE 6

Finally, Lil met a man and was swept off her feet when Angel was six. He was handsome with black hair, blue eyes, side burns like Elvis, and he treated her like a queen. Because he owned his own business he was very wealthy. It was dinner and dancing every week for Lil and Leon.

Lil was what the guys called a brunette beauty. Long brown hair, large beautiful brown eyes, dark skin and around 105 pounds. As beautiful as she was, she still had low self-esteem because of her past with men.

Lil seemed to distance herself from Leon at first until he started to pay more attention to Angel. Then the wall around her started to crumble to the ground. Leon promised Lil that he would help raise Angel and told her she had done such wonderful job raising such a beautiful and smart little girl.

To Lil this was a dream come true - someone who would get her out of the courtyard and into a house. Leon was at their apartment a lot. You could say he lived with them. Their home was nothing to be proud of, Lil kept it clean though. When they started dating, Lil was embarrassed to even bring Leon over to the house. After only a month, it seemed as though he never left except to go to work.

There were finally big dinners every night. Leon would buy the food, and Lil would make what ever he wanted. The cupboards were full, and Lil started to buy clothes for Angel and herself thanks to Leon. It seemed as though things couldn't get any better. Lil started to fall in love. Despite how she felt, everyone that met Leon told her to watch out; something's just not right. She began to distance herself from the family. She thought they were just jealous.

"Lil, why if he has all this money and a house is he moving in with you?" Anne asked.

"Because he doesn't want to rush me into moving to his home and taking Angel away from all her friends. He doesn't just think about us; he puts Angel's needs first. He said after the school year is finished we would move in with him." Lil replied.

Even though Angel had her own bedroom she always slept in her mom's bed with her because she was afraid of the dark. She would sleep right in between her mom and the wall. It wasn't long after dating each other that Leon had a place on the other side of Lil every night. At the time Angel thought the dark was all there was to be afraid of. She found out soon after Leon moved in with them that there was so much more to be afraid of.

Only three months into their relationship things began to change. Leon became more controlling, demanding dinners every night and a clean home. He didn't only change towards Lil; he started to change towards Angel. It all started one night when Angel asked her mom to bring her downstairs to go to the bathroom wearing nothing but her cotton undies and a big t-shirt. Leon volunteered to walk her downstairs.

"Come on sweetie, I will bring you" he said.

Wrapping his hand around Angel's hand, he pulled her out of the bed. On the way down the stairs his hand started to squeeze hers. Then he began to rub the back of her hand with his thumb. She wanted him to let go, but every time she tried to pull her hand away he gave her a glance - one that frightened her.

Angel finished going to the bathroom, came out, and saw Leon sitting on the couch. He tapped his leg and made the gesture for her to come sit on his lap. She refused at first and told him that she wanted to go back upstairs.

"Now come on, I need to talk to you about your mom," he said tapping his knee again.

She started towards him and focused her eyes on a big picture of John Cougar Mellon camp hanging on the wall above his head. He reached for her and asked her for a kiss. She gave him one on the lips, one that a six-year- old would give her new step daddy.

"Give me a good one," he said.

"What do you mean?" she asked.

"Come here Angel give me a good kiss," he ordered and pulled her sixty pound little body onto his lap holding her cheeks and putting his lips on hers and his tongue in her mouth. His rough hand made its way between her legs grabbing and squeezing her thigh.

"Move your tongue around in my mouth" he said. "Don't tell anyone our secret."

Then they walked upstairs to bed and went to sleep. There were more and more of those kisses when Angel was just six.

One night, after the same kind of trip to the bathroom, after going back to bed, Lil fell asleep before Angel did. Angel heard the sheets wrestling around and felt Leon's hand coming towards her and around her mom's waist. He placed his hand on Angel's tummy. No one knows how at that age Angel knew, but she could tell it wasn't right what he was doing. He moved his hand from her tummy and put it between her thighs. He spread her very thin little legs and went into her cotton undies. His fingers started pulling and spreading her pee pee apart causing her a lot of pain. After that night, this became a regular thing that happened. Angel would cry when she heard her mom outside telling friends that she loved the way Leon held her until she fell asleep and wrapped his arms around her till she woke up.

All that year Angel went to school with her friends and pretended nothing was wrong, pretended to have a normal life. One day Ms. Little called her mom to schedule a teacher and parent conference. Angel sat in a chair behind them and kept her head down on the desk. She kept her head down so long that her face became cold against the hard wood. She knew if the teacher had to talk with your parents it must mean that you did something wrong. She didn't know what it could be, because she was always good for Ms. Little. She started to doze off when all of a sudden she heard the words "stay back".

"Angel seems as though she is busy with other things besides her work, she continues to nod off during class" Ms. Little said.

"She loves school, I don't know what is with her, she talks about you all the time" Lil replied.

"I believe she should stay back in the first grade," said Ms. Little.

Angel started to cry. She knew if she stayed back she would have to go to another first grade teacher's room. Her name was Mrs. Lung, and everyone knew she was really mean.

"Can I please stay with you Ms. Little, I promise I will try harder," Angel begged.

"Well I don't see why not, I will try to work something out" she answered.

It was almost summer time and her seventh birthday was almost here. Her dad called the first week in April and said he would be coming down in a few days that he had something real special for her birthday. Like other small children she imagined things that he could bring her. She sat on the end of her bed and pictured her dad walking into her room with his arms wide open, and he would bend down and pick her up.

"Sweetie, daddy has come to bring you and your mom to my home where you will be safe," he would say.

He would help pack her things up, and Leon would walk in, and her dad would push him down and yell, "Leave them alone". They would walk out the door and never return.

In reality, he came and brought her a dog. It was so cute with black and white, curly fur. He didn't weigh more than ten pounds. She named him China after her China dolls. He said he got it because she seemed lonely and sad all the time.

"Dad could I talk to you out there," pointing to the outside.

"Angel hold on before you go anywhere, come here and I will give you some money if you're going with your dad" Leon said from the other room.

Angel walked towards him while her dad waited near the door.

"Angel here is five dollars," he said while coming towards her cheek as if to give her a kiss goodbye.

"Angel remember our little secret. If anyone finds out, I might have to take your mom away from you forever," he whispered in her ear.

Then she walked towards her dad, and they walked down to the store around the corner. She wanted to tell her dad so bad what Leon was doing to her, but if she did then she would never see her mom again.

"Angel what is the matter? Why are you so sad all the time?" he asked.

"Oh nothing daddy, my teacher says I have to stay back that's all," Angel answered.

"Don't worry about that. Have a fun summer then work real hard when you go back to school, but don't let staying back ruin your whole summer. You know I stayed back in the first grade, and I felt smarter than anyone in my class because I already knew a lot of the things they didn't know. You will be just fine. Try to cheer up and show daddy that special Angel smile you have," he said.

Leon hated China simply for the fact that Brad brought this dog into his home without asking him first. Every time that he would get mad at

Angel or Lil, he took his aggression out on China by yelling, stomping, or hitting him. He would get a thrill out of seeing China back into the kitchen corners out of fear while he stomped his foot.

One day Angel came home from a friend's house and when she opened the door she could hear China crying. She looked all over the house for him. Then she heard him near the clothes washer. As she got closer and closer she knew that's where he was. She opened the lid and there he was all wet. She picked him up only to hear him cry in pain. She held him close and dried him off. She ran upstairs and got her blanket from her bed and wrapped him in it and then ran next door to her aunt's house to get her mom. After explaining, crying and screaming at her mom about what happened, they rushed home. Lil told her that China probably got stuck in there looking for food, and there must have been some water left over from her doing laundry earlier. Angel knew what had happened to China- Leon tried to drown him. China seemed to be a fighter though, but he did walk backwards for weeks after and cried when ever someone patted him. Lil didn't dare to bring him to the vet's because doing that would have cost money, and they knew Leon wouldn't give them any for that reason. China only lived for a couple of months after that. Leon said that he didn't see him when he backed up over him with his truck. Leon saw how upset Angel was over China dying and started to bring animals home after that only to let her get close to them before he would torture them in front of her. This seemed to become a game to him; a game that would punish Lil and Angel

My Special Gift

As I sit looking back at my life when I was a little girl
I can't recall many material things to be thankful for
We were noted as one of the worst dressed families in town
Cause we lived on others hand me downs
At school the kids would make fun and call me names
And laugh when I'd hold my head down in shame
In games I'd always be last
And it'd be someone else's turn real fast
I remember being asked to my neighbor's birthday party
I felt privileged she invited me
We ate cake and ice-cream, played games and sung happy birthday
Then she unwrapped the most beautiful baby-doll I've ever seen
I asked if I could hold her, she said yes but not too long
My mom said she's a gift that's meant especially for me
Birthdays and Christmas's would go by, and oh how I'd cry
I just didn't understand where that baby doll could be
The one that was meant especially for me
Each and every night I'd get down on my knees
And pray to the Lord to find a special baby for me
I remember one night getting up from my knees
And asking mama if she thought the Lord was too busy to bother with
me
As she bent down and gave me a good night kiss
She whispered I'm sure your prayers are at the top of his list
The time has finally come and I thank you Lord for
Answering my prayer
I realize now you really did care
You saved the most special baby-doll just for me
A little girl named Summer Marie
By: Lillian

Sister Summer

AGE 7 AND 8

After only six months with Leon, Lil found out that she was pregnant. She couldn't wait to tell Angel that she would soon have a sister or brother. Angel was happy about this, now she would have a sibling like all of her friends.

After finding out about the pregnancy, Leon became very distant from Lil. He would leave for days at a time. Sometimes a week or two would go by without him coming home. After all that had happened, Angel didn't mind him leaving and staying away because this meant she would be able to get sleep without being touched. When he did stay over, he didn't miss a beat. No matter how long he was gone when he returned he expected the house to be spotless and his dinners to be on time. Lil had to rush to the hospital on a few occasions because after their fights she would bleed. Then she'd worry that she was losing the baby.

Lil was only six months along when the doctors told her that she needed to be on bed rest or she would lose the baby. The doctor mentioned that she may be having a hard time because of the stress in her life, and if she has stress than so does the baby. She knew that this wouldn't be an option, so she promised the doctor that she would try and take it easy. Angel helped her in doing everything around the house.

One day in June the heat was supposed to reach a hundred degrees and Leon said that he would be home early, and he better have clean clothes to wear. Lil woke up at seven that morning to start the laundry, hoping that she would hang it on the line by the time it reaches a hundred. She had only one more load to do by noon, and she walked outside to hang it. Angel carried the basket out for her and started to hand her the pins. She watched as the sweat began to cover her mom's face and saw how she would hold her stomach in pain with every reach. All of a sudden Lil started to sway back and forth then she fell to the ground hitting her head on a rock and started to bleed. Angel ran and got Anne next door. They both ran out to Lil who was still unconscious. Anne ran back indoors to call the ambulance. Lil was released from the hospital the very same day and told again that she would have to be on total bed rest. That night was the first time Leon hit Lil across the face for refusing to make him dinner and begging him to order Angel and himself some food.

Before long, Lil started to wear long sleeve shirts and sunglasses to cover her bruises. One day when she wasn't expecting company she thought it was safe to walk around in just her sleeveless nightgown. Anne came over to help with the house work and she noticed all the bruises on Lils arms and legs.

"Lil what is going on, where did all those bruises come from? Is that jerk hitting you? I told you that he was no good in the beginning. You can't let him get away with doing this to you," Anne said.

"Anne it's not what you think. After getting pregnant I became anemic, and I don't have enough iron in my system. I bruise real easy. Even if I bump lightly into something there will be this big bruise the very next day," she lied.

Anne left the house believing what Lil had said and never questioned her again.

Angel finally got a baby sister; Summer was born on August 10, 1980. Lil had to stay in the hospital a little longer than other moms. The doctors said she had a nervous break down because she and the baby were under so much stress. Angel stayed with a friend of Lil's until the day her mom and baby sister came home. The day that Lil came home with Summer Angel didn't leave her baby sister's side. She was so beautiful. Her eyes were like blueberries; her skin was real dark like her mom's, and she had black silky hair like some of Angel's baby dolls. Everything seemed almost perfect until they walked over towards their apartment and saw Leon standing in the door way. He stood almost like a sculpture holding a dozen of long stem roses.

"Lil things are going to be different, I want to make this work," Leon said.

"Angel, isn't that so nice of Leon to be here for us when we got home, and don't worry, he is still going to love you, the same as he loves Summer," Lil said.

Leon bent down and gave Angel a hug and whispered in her ear.

"Now I have someone else to give my special kisses to right Angel" he said.

Angel knew exactly what he meant when he said that. She knew that it now would be her job to watch over her baby sister so Leon couldn't get her. There were some nights that Angel would close her eyes but still stay awake to make sure Leon didn't get up and touch Summer the way he touches her. She would go to school the next day and fall asleep at her desk or stay home pretending that she was sick if Leon didn't go to work.

One night he became sick of the same kisses and during Angels nightly trip to the bathroom that Leon demanded he had to take her to he held her against the bathroom door. After her special kisses he usually would let her go but this time it was different. He pulled his pants down revealing his penis. Angel turned away and he pulled her face towards this monstrous thing.

"Angel kiss it, kiss it the same way you kiss me stick out your tongue" he whispered.

"No I don't want to" she began to cry.

"Don't worry it won't hurt I promise"

She stuck out her tongue and he put his penis on the end of it and then past her teeth. He forced it in and out, and then it began to get harder and harder. Finally he stopped for a second and as she had this thing in her mouth she looked up at him with her baby brown eyes hoping he would find sympathy towards her. He finished in her mouth the liquid began to rush down her throat and she could feel her supper began to make its way up to meet the salty sticky mess. She threw up on his penis and all over the floor.

"What the fuck are you thinking" he took a hand full of her hair and forced her face into her own vomit on the floor. Rubbing her nose into it as if he were punishing a dog for peeing on the floor. "Don't think for a minute I'm going to clean that mess up, you make it disappear the same way you made it appear" After that she knew she was nothing more than an animal and she never let a drop of that stuff leave her mouth again.

After only a few months Summer had become very ill and cried a lot. Lil took her to the doctors, and it turned out she had two very bad ear infections. When Leon had come home later that night Lil told him what was wrong with Summer and she asked him for some money.

"I'm not a fucking bank you know. Now here's a twenty for the medicine," he yelled.

Lil then went door to door asking people if she could borrow the rest

13

of the money for the medicine. After finding a babysitter for Summer and Angel, she went to get the medicine and then to Leon's garage to talk to him about the way he was acting.

The next time Lil came home Angel screamed when she saw her mom. There was blood all over her. She had cuts on her arms and neck. When Libby the babysitter asked her where the blood and cuts came from, all she would say about it was that he was mad because the medicine cost so much, so he threw the medicine bottles at her. Being without medicine that night all Summer did was cry.

The next day Lil had to ask around the neighborhood if anyone had any amoxicillin for Summer. Someone told Lil she could probably tell welfare about her money situation, and they might be able to help her. Lil rushed down to welfare and pleaded with them to help her. It wasn't much but they gave her money to pay rent, a little food and medicine for the kids if they needed it. It is strange that when you are under someone's control for so long, getting help from the state seems almost like freedom. She no longer had to ask for Leon's help as much as before.

They still ran out of food a lot because of the meals that Leon demanded to have every night. There were a lot of fights over food and money, both of which he had plenty and they had none. There were also a lot of cuts on Lil from those fights.

When these fights happened Angel would leave the house and bring Summer around to all of her friends so that they could see her. She would treat her like she was her very own porcelain doll. She was not only very beautiful but she was smart also, she learned things very quickly. She was only nine months old when she began to walk.

Angel noticed that she would have a lot of rashes on the many occasions that she changed her. She would also cry every time Angel would try to take off her diaper. There were times that Leon would change her, but he insisted that he did this in her crib upstairs. One time Angel walked up after Leon to watch him. She walked in the bedroom as he was changing Summer and he turned around and told her to get out. She left but snuck back in to watch him Summer was screaming while his hands were down between her legs, and she was squeezing her little legs together. Angel knew what he was doing to her because he did the same to her so many times before. After that Angel tried not to leave her sister's side, and the times that Leon wanted to change her Angel would scream in a raging fit.

Lil didn't understand what was the matter with Angel-why was she so out of control. Lil asked her friends why they thought Angel acted the way she did. Almost every one of them told her that it was normal behavior.

"Lil, Angel wants to be the one to help change Summer. If Leon does it than he isn't paying attention to her the way she wants him to," Libby said.

There were a lot of nights when Angel would wake up under Summer's crib, cold and tired, but this way she knew Leon didn't touch Summer that night.

Summer began to talk at the young age of just six months. It wasn't long before she would yell "NO" or "STOP" at Leon as he would hit her mom. Angel would hug and hold her hands over Summer's ears and they would sit in the kitchen corner for hours as the fight went on. There were times Summer would slip out of Angel's arms and run over to tug on Lil's pant legs trying to pull her away from Leon. He would always take her and sit her down very hard on Angel's lap again and again.

First Time She Told

AGE 9 AND 10

"Angel honey has anyone ever touched your private area?" Lil asked Angel when she was nine.

She answered but was very frightened because she knew it was a secret.

"Yes"

"Who?"

"Leon touches me when you're sleeping."

"How many times did he do this?"

"Every night almost."

Lil started to cry and held Angel's hands as her whole body began to shake out of control. Angel became more frightened when she noticed the blood dripping from her mom's nose and the veins pulsing from her forehead.

"I promise I will make sure he never touches my baby girl again, understand me Angel?"

Then in what seemed like seconds, the door downstairs slammed shut. Leon was home.

"You stay right here, I will be right back," Lil said holding Angel down on the bed.

"Momma please don't. He said that he will take you away from me if I told you" Angel said holding her mom's hands.

Then Lil was out the door and left Angel on the bed wondering what will happen next. Angel pulled the covers over her head and prayed to God as she listened to the screaming back and forth between her mom and Leon.

"Angel told me everything! Get out and never come back here or I will call the police," she said.

Then there was a big slapping noise and she knew her mom had been hit again.

"How can you listen to a child over me after everything that I have done for you two?" Leon responded.

Yet in his next breath Leon admitted that he had a problem and said it wouldn't happen again. Angel cried when she heard her mom tell Leon to talk to her and apologize, letting her know that it wouldn't happen again.

After a lot of blood and a black eye, Lil didn't question him about what he had done to Angel for a while. But when Angel was ten the question came up again. Angel heard yelling and screaming downstairs. Some of it sounded like Summer's. She ran downstairs and saw Summer sitting in the corner of the kitchen. She was only three at the time, so Angel again put her on her lap and held her ears tight to keep her from hearing the screams. They watched as Leon hit their mom over and over across the face with his fist. They watched with fear as the blood shot from her nose and mouth nearly hitting them across the room.

"I'll call the police!" she yelled.

"Don't you know by now I own the police!" he yelled as he wrapped his hands around her neck.

Her face started to turn white then a light blue. She couldn't breathe. Angel jumped up and ran across the room only to feel a slap across her head throwing her down. He slammed her mom against the counter and picked up the toaster and hit her in the head with it. She fell to the floor and stayed down for what seemed like forever. He just kept kicking her and yelling. She came to after a few more kicks to the stomach. After an hour or so, everything went back to normal. No one was talking, and they all went to bed. The thing that wasn't normal was her mom's face- beaten up and bruised and one of her eyes nearly swollen shut.

The next day Angel was told to baby-sit Summer almost all day while Lil and Leon were in the bedroom. Later that night when they came out it seemed as though they had made up because Leon brought all of them out to eat. Its true make up can cover pain, Lil had so much on her face that you could hardly see the bruises. Lil didn't mention him hurting Angel again until they were on the way home. The fight seemed to have gotten to her, and she brought it up again.

"Leon if you ever lay your hands on me again I will call the police" she firmly said.

"You had to ruin the night didn't you? Are you really bringing this up again? You have to know by now that I own the police. What about the kids? Say that you get your way, and the police come and tell me to leave. Then I'll bring you to court and get custody of Summer. I'll prove that you are unfit, and you will lose everything including your kids. Angel would go to her dad's, that is if he wants her," he said.

Time and time again Leon threatened Lil, telling her he would kill her children. Laying on the cold kitchen floor after a strong hit to the face, he told her that he was married years ago, and when his wife accused him of molesting his own daughter, he buried them where the cops would never look.

The very first time that Leon was gone; Lil went to the police station and asked them if they could do a search for one Rhonda and Tommy, Leon's children. After a few weeks went by, the police reached Lil at the number she gave them and told her that there were two children born under those names at the hospital in Lincoln. They couldn't be traced anywhere at that time. That's when Lil knew she would have to find a way out because her family would be the next not to be found.

The landlord wanted to clean up the apartments that were in the courtyard and placed Lil, Angel, and Summer into an apartment down the road. While moving, Lil thought it was the time to make a change and kick Leon out. When he left, Leon put a number in Lil's hands, and she didn't waste anytime calling the number.

"Hello," a woman answered.

"Yes, hello, my name is Lillian, and I just kicked my boyfriend out and before leaving he handed me your number."

"What is his name?"

"Leon. We've been together for almost five years. How do you know him?"

"Well you fucking bitch, my name is Leonna, and we've been together for four years, so I know you're lying! Plus we have a daughter together, and she's three."

"You don't have to believe me because I don't want the son of a bitch any longer! I have the best thing from him, her name is Summer and she's also three."

Leon decided to go live with Leonna, her ten year old daughter Kinsley, and their baby Kristina. Angel knew that if Leon had another stepdaughter he was probably touching her also. Angel wanted to meet this other little girl. Did she feel as sad as she did? Was her mom bruised and crying all the time like her mom?

Lil started to become jealous of Leon's other family and begged for him to come back. He would make an appearance every now and then and would wait for Lil to go to sleep. Since Angel no longer slept in her mother's bed, he would sneak into her room to make sure she was still under his control and body. Angel fought him more than ever as the touching began to get harder and harder.

"Fight all you want, but if you tell any of our secrets again, I will kill your mom and be able to touch your sissy any time I want. You know your dad don't want you. He has his own family now, so you'll have to stay with me."

After that she didn't put up the usual fight when he put his fingers in her. The usual touching seemed to become boring to him, so he started to do something different. He made her put her hands under her butt, and then he put his tongue and mouth on her vagina. He kept saying over and over again how she was now becoming such a big girl. It didn't hurt as much as the fingers did, and she begged for him to only do this because the fingers hurt so much.

"I will do what I goddamn want to do; you don't tell me what to do!" he said and within a minute he had three fingers in her.

As tears started to roll down her face, he demanded she smile and stop being such a baby. He finally got up, left, and went back to her mom's room where she could hear the bed hitting the wall for hours. She sat up and prayed that her mom would find someone else.

This prayer finally came true a few months later. Her mom started to see another man, one that they had known for a few years. The relationship didn't last long; Leon paid someone to bust out all the windows of his car and home. After the boyfriend left for good, Leon began to come over more often, but for only his benefit. Angel would sit and cry while listening to her mom scream "stop" or "get off please" for hours from her bedroom.

Angel and Summer shared a bedroom and Angel would take Summer into their room and hug her and tell her a story of angels or fairies that someday would help all of them to find a place to hide from him. As Summer slept, the yelling would continue long into the night. When it finally stopped, Leon would finish with their mom and come into their bedroom to say good bye to Summer and give her a kiss on the cheeks. Angel always wondered why he didn't see the tears running down Summer's cheeks the way she did-the ones he caused by hurting their mommy-or-maybe he did see and just didn't care.

Leon finally made his way back into Lil's bed for good. Every time she kicked him out, he would beg, plead, and promise to change. Lil would accept him back and stop seeing other people. The hitting would stop, at least for awhile, but it never lasted long. Again, Lil would kick him out, and again, he would worm his way back in. This became their usual routine happening over and over and over again.

Three months went by, and Leon brought a dog home with him one day for Summer. They named her Sandy. She was a tan lab almost big enough for Summer to ride. She was a wonderful dog, and Summer loved her so much. Sandy would cry with them during the fights and especially after Leon took his anger out on her instead of hitting Lil. Leon would have a grin on his face when Sandy would pee on the floor after one of these arguments. He could then feel strong and powerful by dragging her down the stairs by her tail into the back yard, as if it were her fault for staining the rug with piss.

During the summer Sandy became pregnant from one of the dogs upstairs. When it was time for her to deliver she had a rough time, two of the six puppies didn't make it. Lil and Angel decided to bury the puppies in the back yard. After coming home and seeing the mess that Sandy had left from the births Leon let them know that the remaining puppies would only be staying for the short time of three weeks.

"That's enough shitting all over the place," he said.

Three weeks went by, and they found all of them nice homes. Sandy cried a lot when the puppies were gone. Her stomach still seemed to hurt as it swelled up with milk. Angel would sit for hours and massage her belly to try and ease the crying. Leon took her pain to his advantage one night. Lil started yelling at him to make his own dinner if he wanted it right. Sandy was lying at Angel's feet.

"You would have more time to cook my food if you didn't take care of that fuckin dog all the time!" he yelled.

Then he kicked Sandy in the stomach so hard that she threw up her food and peed all over the carpet. Angel ran to the bathroom to get a towel knowing that Sandy would be dragged outside if the mess wasn't cleaned up in time. To her horror while cleaning the pee, she noticed blood mixed in. Angel stayed up all night with her to make sure she didn't die like her babies. Lil brought Sandy to the veterinarian's and she never came home.

Leon beat up Lil really bad that night, and she finally went to the police, telling them what he had done to Angel and herself. They asked her if she wanted to press charges and she asked them how long he be in jail. They replied probably only the night, and then there would be a court date where they would have to testify against him. She became too scared and left the police station and went home.

Later that night Leon told them that he heard from a friend that they were at the police station. Lil pretended to ignore him and continued to iron their clothes.

"They asked us a lot of questions, but we didn't answer them," Angel said.

"I know everywhere you two go because I have enough money to find you-no matter where you are!" he yelled.

"Leave her alone! Just go take a shower; you smell," Lil said under her breath.

"What was that? You went to the police, and now you think you are tough and want to talk back. We'll see how tough you are." He stood up and grabbed the iron and threw it at the television. Glass went everywhere, and then he stomped out of the room. Lil fell to the floor and on her hands and knees picking up the glass, so Summer wouldn't pick any up and get hurt. Angel went to help her and Leon came back in and told her to get her ass into their room and don't come out. Angel turned around just in time to see him push her mom's shoulders down making her hands go onto the glass.

"Don't you ever talk back to me in front of my daughter."

Later he left for the night, but Angel still didn't dare to come out even when she heard his car drive away.

The Shelter

AGE 11

While Leon was gone Lil laughed and had fun with her friends and family. They were almost like a real family. They hoped that he would never return, but only three weeks went by before he came back. The laughter turned into tears, and the fun crumbled to fear.

The school year was almost done, and soon Angel would be going into the middle school. With everything going on at home, school was her savior. But she knew that going to a new school meant she would have to make new friends.

The elementary school that she was in decided that they needed a counselor, someone that would take the heat off the nurse and that everyone could talk to. All of the kids wanted to see what this new person looked like.

"Angel, I heard that she was a real shrink, a lady that could read your mind," Joe said tapping his head on the desk.

"No one can read someone's mind. That's just what they show on tv stupid," Angel slapped her head and left the room.

Then there was the counselor walking down the hall towards Angel. She wanted to turn and run before this woman did read her mind, yet she was curious about her. She looked nice and trusting. You know that kind of person you meet and you know you could tell her just about anything.

One morning, after the pledge of the allegiance, the counselor began calling fifth grade students to her office one at a time. Angel waited in her chair very patiently for her turn, thinking of what she might tell her. Leon's not around and she would be the only one in the room with her; she wondered if she could tell her what he does to her and her mom. This was her chance to tell someone. What would the harm be? She could get it off her chest then move onto middle school and never see this woman again. The next thing she knew she was sitting across from her and thinking of all the things Leon had done to her.

"Angel, do you have any siblings at home?"

"Yes, I have a sister. Her name is Summer, and she lives with me, and I have a brother whose name is Colby and a sister whose name is Katrina. They live with my real dad in Connecticut."

"Do you have a stepdad, or is it just you, your mom and your sister at home?"

Angel's eyes started to fill up with tears and she hadn't even told her what happened at home yet. She realized that this may be her only chance to tell someone other than her mom.

"Yes, his name is Leon, and my mom has been with him since I was six," Angel answered.

She looked around and noticed that it was just them in the room. Her hands began to sweat as she rubbed the leather on the chair under her. Just as she was about to tell her everything, the door swung open, it was the principal.

"Ms. Newton, you have a phone call on line two," he announced.

She put her hand on Angels knee and told her it was very nice to meet her and good luck in the sixth grade, you may go back to class now. Angel's head dropped down towards the floor as she walked towards the door. Maybe she didn't need to know what went on at her house she thought.

Angel ran to the girls' bathroom and into a stall, slamming the door behind her. As she sat on the back of the toilet making sure no one could see her feet, she began to cry. The smell of the blue water coming up to meet her nose began to make her nauseous. What if that was her only chance left to tell someone before he killed her mom and her? She sat in that bathroom until the three o'clock bell rang and no one came looking for her. This didn't surprise her no-one cared.

It was only a couple of weeks until her eleventh birthday, and her dad called to tell her that he would be coming to the house to give her a gift that she has wanted for awhile. If only he knew that all she wanted was for him to help her mom, Summer, and herself and take them away.

It was the day of her birthday, and she sat at the window while a party with the family went on all around her.

"Mom, he said he would be here today"

"Angel, if he said he would be here today, then he will be here today. Come and make a wish, and blow the candles out on your cake."

Angel did what her mom asked and rushed right back to the window again.

With every person who walked out the door another tear came rolling down her cheeks. Over and over again she blew on the window and spelled out daddy, hoping that he would see this when he came towards the house. Everyone left after a couple of hours, and the sun began to go down. She didn't recall falling asleep but she woke up the next morning on the floor under that same window with a blanket around her and a pillow under her head.

Brad called a couple days later and told Angel that Colby was sick and he would be down tomorrow. He brought her a boom box to play her tapes in. Angel sat on the floor changing the dials of the box and listening to her favorite station. As she sat there she waited and hoped to hear sorry from her dad for not coming on her birthday, but Denise complained that she had a headache from the drive, and they left only after an hour or so. Brad didn't have an apology for not coming on time, and it seemed that now he didn't even have his own mind. He was completely under Denise's control.

That night Leon kept Lil in the bedroom for hours. "Go ahead and tell me that bastard was better than me! I saw how you looked at him you ungrateful bitch!"

"Please Leon, don't do this. He came to see Angel not me. I love you and only you," Lil said as she begged for him to stop.

The steel bed post slammed over and over against the wall and with every hit. Angel could hear her mom cry and yell stop.

Leon came out after Angel was already in bed, and she heard her door open. The clock next to her bed read 2:05 am. She laid still and pretended to be asleep, but he shook her over and over again. He stopped shaking her long enough to pick up Summer and bring her to her mom's bed. Leon told Angel that he wanted to give her a birthday present. She thought, wow, she didn't even ask him for anything.

Leon took her pajama pants off and took her hand and put it on his penis; he then unzipped his pants and pulled her underwear off. One finger went into her and then with her body hesitating another finger went into her. Her vagina began to burn, and it hurt so bad. Her hand was still on his penis and tears were running down her face.

"Don't you cry? I could make it worse than this. Stop those tears now!"

Angel wiped her tears away and watched as the sweat began to drip from his black greasy hair and onto her nose. His penis was getting hard, and he pulled down his pants and pushed his penis into her vagina. With every thrust he would say, "Happy birthday Angel."

She then let her mind take her somewhere else. This was the first time she had an out of body experience. She was on the beach with friends, laughing and having a good time. When Leon finally finished and she came back to reality, the inside of her legs were all wet. Yet instead of being mad or upset like she should've been, she was embarrassed because she thought she had peed herself.

"Happy Birthday. Now you're a woman, and you can clean up this fucking mess you made under yourself," then he walked out.

She got up to go to the bathroom three times within the hour, when she went to the bathroom her vagina burned when she peed. She was so scared because there was blood mixed with her pee on the toilet paper and the last time she saw anything like that was when Sandy's pee came out bloody the night she never returned from the vets.

Leon left at about 3:00 am, and Angel went to tell her mom that she was bleeding out of her pee hole. Lil hugged her and explained to her about a woman's period.

"But momma it hurts when I go to the bathroom."

"Angel that's normal. Just take this warm washcloth and put it into your underwear, it will feel better in the morning," then she sent Angel to bed.

As she began to fall asleep her body was falling asleep also for the first time that night. But as her eyes closed all she could see were his eyes looking at her. How could her mom not know that Leon had hurt her she thought?

The pain stayed for three more days. It finally stopped hurting just about the same night Leon came and took Angel for a ride with him to the garage.

"Angel lay down on the seat, put your legs up and open them."

She laid down and did what he had asked without question.

"Jesus Angel! Take off your pants. Don't be so fucking stupid all the time. You're just like your mother-never thinking"

"But how about if we get in an accident or something and I don't have my pants on? I will get into trouble."

"Just do what I tell you to and don't worry about it."

Being naive at the time and thinking people outside will know something was wrong. She kept her fingers on the back window hoping someone would call the police.

"Angel you should be proud that I give you all of this attention. Most step-dads don't devote this much time to their step-kids. Look at your own father, he is never around because he knows I treat you good," he said.

Then with a sudden push two fingers were inside her. She clinched her other hand on the smelly leather seats. She told him for the first time that it hurt really bad when he did that. He gave her a look and grinned.

"You know all fathers do this if they really love their daughters. They get them ready for marriage or other men that way the men won't hurt you when they fuck you," he said.

In her heart she knew this wasn't true. Her real dad never did this to her, but maybe he doesn't love her, and he does this to Katrina. Should she thank Leon for doing this, she thought?

As they got closer to the garage he told her to get up. She was there to help him count all of his money. They went upstairs, and there was money all over the bed. There must have been thousands of dollars to count. When the money was counted and put in a drawer, he told her to lie down. He put his mouth all over her vagina, and he told her how good it tastes this time and handed her two hundred dollar bills. At the age of eleven she was being used as a prostitute, and this money was hush money. She never had any money like that before to spend, and she knew he would have done it anyway, so she took the money.

Leon then walked her outside so she could help him cut wood, but Angel's vagina hurt, throbbing with pain with every step she took. As the sun began to beat down between her legs; she began to sweat.

They finally went home when it got to dark to cut wood, but Leon didn't go in. He just dropped Angel off at the door. Lil looked sad, and Angel began to get nervous, thinking that maybe she knew that Leon had given her the money.

"Angel, go to your room and get some clothes for you and Summer."

After everything was packed up, the three of them started down the hill. Angel started to shake as she realized they were getting closer and closer to the police station. As soon as they walked into the police station a police officer approached them. You could tell that Lil had already called them. As Lil went into one room, Angel and Summer were instructed to stay on a long cushioned bench in another room. Lil came out of the room and they all got into a police car and drove and drove.

The next time Angel opened her eyes it was daylight, and they were in a big city surrounded by huge, tall buildings. There was a lady with them who brought them out to eat at Burger King. Angel told her that she didn't eat meat before the Lady ordered anything.

"You may have to get used to eating whatever it is when other people are buying it for you," she said.

Angel sat at the table with a cheeseburger in front of her. The smell of it made her stomach turn. As she looked up, she saw the Lady watching her, so she took a huge bite- hoping that with just one she could finish it. She ran into the bathroom and threw it all up.

The same day, they ended up at a place that looked like an apartment building. The Lady called it a shelter for battered women. Angel looked at Lil hoping for some explanation and that is exactly what she got.

"We'll be staying here for a while to get away from Leon, and we won't go home until he's gone," she said.

The first night they were there it was hard. All Summer did was cry, asking for her Daddy. (she was only four at the time). Summer also cried because she was really hungry. All Lil could say was that they would eat again when it was light out. Then they all crammed into a twin size bed because that was all that was available.

The next morning finally came, and they got up and walked into the other room. There were a lot of people just sitting there watching TV. There weren't many kids, it was mostly grown-ups. Angel stayed in the room holding Summer's hand so that she wouldn't run off while Lil went downstairs and came back a few minutes later.

"We have to go to town for money. It's not a long walk and maybe if we see a park we will stop," she said.

Angel thought the townspeople were so different than the people she knew from home. There were kids her age just walking around by themselves. Some ladies had cups asking for money; some men were under cardboard boxes just sleeping, and some would hold onto their things as Angel and Lil walked by-as if they would steal from them.

They ended up inside a big building-the biggest one Angel had ever seen. Everywhere inside there were women with crying children. They were at the welfare office. Lil began to beg them to help her and her kids. Within only a couple days, they finally received food stamps, and in the meantime the shelter let them eat there.

As she watched Lil ask people for shelter and food, Angel realized that what pride Lil once had was all gone. It was all given up for them. Lil would do anything to keep Angel and Summer fed and warm. Every time she walked through that food line her eyes would start to fill up with tears, and she would turn to her kids and smile.

The longest two weeks went by without Leon hitting, yelling, or touching any of them. They all felt safe at least for the moment. However, Lil never seemed happy. It seemed as though she began to miss him. One night a lady came into the room and told Lil that she had a call.

"Nobody knows where I am," she said to the lady.

"He says it's an emergency," the women yelled.

"Oh my god! He must have gotten to Anne, he knows that is the only way that I would come back," she said almost to herself, but everyone in the room heard her.

When she came back, she took Angel's hand and held it so tight hoping that it would stop her from shaking.

"Angel he found us. We have to go back," she said.

Angel knew who she meant. They packed their things. By morning they were back home and there he was, just sitting in the living room with flowers for Lil and hugs for all of them-like nothing ever happened.

"Thank god you're all back. I was so worried," he said.

He left Angel alone only for a couple of weeks. Then it was like before; he would pay her a visit late at night while her mom slept. He would do the same things over and over again. It felt as though her vagina was ripping apart sometimes. When she would try to stop him, he would just go harder and harder. It was as if he was paying her back for taking his family away from him.

How did he find us? Angel asked herself this question over and over again. The only people who knew where they were, were the police and that woman that brought them to Burger King. If he could find them there then he would be able to find them anywhere.

After a few months went by the police moved them again. This time it was into someone's house. Angel didn't mind it because the lady who owned the house had a girl around Summer's age. This kept Summer busy and happy because she now had someone to play with. But, they didn't stay long since Lil didn't like the fact they were staying at someone else's house, and so they again went back to Leon. It was almost as if Lil couldn't get enough of him. Once they were back home Angel paid the price for them leaving.

The Best Summer

AGE 12

After arriving back home there were new families that had moved in upstairs and in the back part of the building.

The family that lived behind them had two girls and one boy. Arlene who was ten was the oldest. Virginia was the same age as Summer, and Prescott, the only boy, was the youngest.

In the front of the building there was Claudia who was the cool, girly, vibrant, older sister. The second oldest, Audrey, was the tomboy and perpetually angry. Miller was a typical annoying, horny, teenage brother and was third in line. The youngest, Marcia, was always sad. She was a follower who would do anything to fit in with the crowd.

Claudia was Angel's age, She was the one that Angel would wear make up for because she was someone Angel wanted to impress. Without even knowing it, she was also the one that taught Angel to be girly. Angel watched her every move, especially how her curves would slide with her clothing as she walked. With long blonde hair and big blue eyes you couldn't take your eyes off her.

Claudia and Angel hung out almost everyday, but after awhile it seemed as though she grew up a lot faster than Angel did. So, Angel began to hang out with Audrey, even though she wasn't anything like her. There were things about Audrey, however, that Angel admired: like the way she didn't care how people looked at her, and the way she stood up for Angel when someone picked a fight with her.

Since Audrey was more tomboy than girl, her wardrobe consisted of nothing but jeans and raggedy t-shirts. She always asked Angel who she was trying to impress and tell her that she didn't need to dress up everywhere they went. Angel realized that she had become a vision of

Claudia, and Audrey hated it almost as much as Angel did, but Angel didn't know how to change.

Angel shopped at the Salvation Army for almost all her clothes and made the best out of them. She thought everyone else dressed "poor" and didn't know why they dressed the way they did. So the times Leon gave her hush money for what he was doing to her; she usually bought clothes for her friends. She bought Audrey some clothes thinking she wouldn't dress the way she did if she had better clothes, and while Audrey always accepted them later on Angel would see Marcia wearing them.

Angel considered the hush money dirty because of the way she had gotten it. It was very seldom that she spent the money on herself and being generous with her friends allowed her to spend the money without the guilt that she associated with it.

At the beginning of the summer Claudia began a crew for girls only, and of course Angel, Audrey, and Arlene were in this crew. They decided they needed a place to hold their meetings that they planned on having, and they made a fort out back in the woods. They needed a lookout for some of the bad things that they planned on doing and Marcia was excited to step in. Marcia would tell them right away when someone was coming and this would give Claudia time to put out her cigarette.

On occasion Miller would try to sneak in on their fun, but Angel and Claudia weren't having it. Miller was annoying most of the time, but after awhile he became like Angel's little brother, so she wanted to stick up for him and let him in on some of the fun. He would confess at times how much he loved her and wanted her to be his girlfriend. Angel told him time and time again that he was just too young for her. This made him mad, so he would tell Lil about some of the things that the girls were doing. Consequently, Lil started to watch over Angel a little better when she was in the company of the crew.

Along with being part of the crew there came confidence in meeting new people. That summer Angel became friends with more and more kids. Most of the kids lived on the same hill or close by. When Leon was away or at work all the kids usually hung out at Angel's house. They would tell her that her mom was so much cooler than theirs.

Soon after summer started Lil decided to take up watching Leonna's and Leon's daughter Kris, and Leon's stepdaughter Kinsey was part of the package. Kris and Summer being almost the exact same age seemed to fight every minute. Kinsey, on the other hand, was the perfect daughter in front of all the parents. She wore all the appropriate clothing and said all the appropriate words. Parents knew her as the girl that would change their daughters and sons into perfect children like her. What they didn't know was what she did when she came to Angel's house. She borrowed revealing clothes from all of Angel's friends, found all the parties, and always knew where to find drugs.

Angel had a hard time understanding why her mom kept them for the summer, but she was happy that she did because Kinsey became like a sister to her. Angel also thought if Lil watched the kids then it would somehow keep Leon happy for awhile.

When Angel wasn't with Kinsey she spent a lot of time at Meredith's house up the road. Angel tried to spend almost every night at her new friend Meredith's house, hoping that she could get some rest from the nightly abuse she got from Leon. She also made arrangements for Summer to go to a friend's house for a sleepover. Leon knew exactly what she was doing, and at times became furious Lil would let this go on. He would always make sure Angel remembered the rules.

"Remember, don't tell anyone about our little secret. You know what will happen don't you?"

Meredith and Angel became really close friends. Meredith was so much like Angel. They talked the same and dressed the same, sometimes wearing the exact same outfit that they made.

They started to go to the Lincoln roller skating rink on the weekends. Lil would drop them off and then come and pick them up. Sometimes they took Kinsey with them, but first they made her promise not to tell Lil anything they did. Angel also liked to bring Summer with her. She loved showing off how cute she was, besides she didn't dare leave her alone with Leon.

Angel met her first real boyfriend, Robert, at the rink. When she began dating Robert, Meredith started dating his friend Alvin. It was around May of that year that Robert started to try things with Angel (the same things Leon did all the time). Angel liked Robert a lot, but she was afraid that if she did anything with him Leon would be able to tell. Then Leon would tell Lil and she would get really mad at her and not let her be around the group anymore so Angel wouldn't let Robert do anything. Robert told Angel it was okay, that he loved her and he would wait.

Meredith had already done it with Alvin and they only had been dating for a couple of weeks. Meredith wasn't shy on expressing how good it felt either. Angel became jealous that Meredith had done these things first; Angel began to try a few things with Robert like making out, dry humping, or even letting him feel her up. She never felt comfortable with it, but she let him because all of her other friends told her that they all did it too.

Angel started to love the attention she got, and being on top of Robert made her feel in control. She was finally in charge of her body and she liked it. She even began to feel comfortable at times with Robert, especially when he held her close after an hour long make out session.

While Angel was getting comfortable, Robert was getting antsy. The promise he made to her to wait began to bother him a lot. So, only a couple of months after they started dating Robert decided to go with another girl; one he didn't have to wait for one who gave it up to him the very first night. It hurt Angel a lot, but she liked a lot of other boys, so she got over it really fast.

It was during this time that Angel began to notice things about Meredith's body the way it was filling in and all the curves she had. Her butt was round and stuck out a little over her hip hugger jeans, and when wearing a bra her boobs would meet each other in the middle.

Angel was twelve and still didn't need bras, and she always wore a belt to keep her pants up because there weren't any curves to keep them up. One day while hanging out at the rink a boy called Angel a "carpenter's dream" flat as a board and never been nailed. All of this made Angel ask herself why the boys would want her if they could have someone that looked like Meredith instead. Meredith answered this question for her. She told her that they wanted what they couldn't have and what Angel wasn't giving them was her cherry.

Angel met a boy named Constantine one weekend at the rink; he was standing at the counter that she needed to get her skates from. He came closer to her and asked her to slow skate with him. She told him no at first because of the way he looked. He wasn't anything like the other boys she liked. His hair was short, blonde, and parted on the side, and he had buck teeth. He wore nice slacks with a collared shirt. Angel was into boys who wore ripped jeans and concert t-shirts. Like most girls her age, she was attracted to the bad boy image. She was an average teenager from the 80's and Constantine looked like a teenager from the 60's, so she left him behind with a sad look on his face.

That night things were different for Angel. She tried to talk to Robert, but he ignored her. (She had never been ignored by a guy before). So, when Constantine wouldn't leave her alone she decided to give him a chance.

When he asked her to skate with him for the tenth time she gave in and said yes.

Angel and Constantine skated around, holding hands, most of the night. Every time they went past Robert, Angel looked at him. She hoped it was making him jealous. Robert finally pulled Angel aside and asked her why she was being such a bitch.

"I didn't do anything but skate with Constantine. Why are you jealous?" Angel asked him. Then she skated away and sat down with Constantine. One thing she had learned from Claudia was if you play hard to get, they will want you even more.

"Angel, can I walk you home?" Constantine asked.

"It's about five miles away, but if you want you can walk me home," she said.

She called her mom and told her that a friend was bringing her home. She knew she would be late because walking home would take them a while, but she wasn't ready for Leon.

When they went outside, Constantine admitted that he just wanted to walk her home because he wanted to get to know her without all the other guys around. He gave her his leather-jacket that looked like he borrowed it from his dad-because it was a little cold out.

Constantine then took a glass thing out of his pocket; Angel had never seen a thing that looked like it before. He put a lighter up to it until the stuff inside turned red then he took a deep breathe in. She asked him if she could try it, and he handed it to her. It smelled real funny. She finally asked him what it was and he told her it was pot.

"You've never tried pot before! Where have you been?" he asked.

"I have tried a cigarette before, but it made me choke," she answered.

"This won't make you choke. Pot goes down real smooth. You don't have to inhale a lot, you just suck and blow" he replied.

As he held the lighter up to the pipe, she took a deep breathe, then slowly blew it out. She instantly felt a head rush, and after a few more drags her body went a little numb. She started to think of the hell she was going to get when she got home late and what Leon might do to her, but the thought disappeared with the next puff. Constantine told her that she seemed like a pro because she didn't even cough once, and he had never seen a girl smoke that much. They walked and talked all the way home. He dropped her off in front of her house and kissed her gently on the cheek.

"Will I hear from you ever again?" Angel asked.

"Of course you will sweetie, I'll call you. What's your number?" he replied.

That night Leon never came in. As she laid on her bed, the room felt calm and her body was weak. She kept pinching herself thinking how great it was that it didn't hurt that bad.

Tomorrow felt like it took forever to get there. It was finally light out, but looking at the clock it was only like six or seven in the morning. The phone rang at about eleven. Lil yelled to her and told her that there was a boy on the phone for her. She ran to get the phone and took it into her bedroom and jumped on the bed excitedly knowing who it was.

"Hello sweetie, I told you that I would call. You want to go to the beach today and hang out?" Constantine asked.

She waited for him and he finally showed up around one or two. Unfortunately, Leon pulled in at the same time. With a grin on his face Leon asked Constantine who he was.

"Hello sir, my name is Constantine. It's nice to meet you," Constantine said, and he extended his hand to meet Leon's.

Angel pulled Constantine's other hand and said,

"We have to go. Everyone is waiting for us."

"Now you two behave yourselves," Leon said.

"Angel didn't you tell me that you have a sister around your age?" Constantine asked.

"Yes, her name is Kinsey. She's in the house. If you want to meet her I'll go get her," she answered.

"Yeah, go and get her. She can hook up with my younger brother. He's at the beach waiting to meet you," he said.

When Kinsey came out of the house, Angel introduced her to Constantine and she could tell right away that Kinsey didn't like him because she gave him an evil, disgusted look.

"Kinsey, would you like to go to the beach with us? Constantine has a brother, and we think you two would get along," Angel asked her.

"Yeah, whatever. I have nothing better to do today," she answered.

All the way to the beach Kinsey complained about how hot it was driving Angel and Constantine crazy.

"Kinsey, what exactly were you expecting? It's summer out and that's why we're going to the beach for Christ sake," Constantine spoke up.

They finally got to the beach and met up with Constantine's brother.

"Angel and Kinsey, this is my brother Monroe. Monroe, this is my girl Angel and her sister Kinsey," Constantine said.

Monroe pulled Constantine to the side. The girls could hear everything they said.

"Monroe, isn't Angel a hottie like I said?" Constantine asked.

"Yeah, she is and her sister is too. Look at those tits!" Monroe replied.

Angel thought this would make Kinsey mad, but she just bent her back some and smiled.

They spent the whole day together Angel introduced Constantine and Monroe to all of her friends that were at the beach-even Robert. Later on, during the day, most of them said they thought Constantine was a geek. That was until night came, and he pulled out his pipe. To Angel's surprise everyone knew what it was and smoked it.

On the way home all Kinsey did was talk about Monroe and how gorgeous he was. He had long blonde hair and huge muscles, especially for a twelve year old. He was the average bad boy-nothing like his brother.

Every day for a month or so, Constantine either called or they hung out. They kissed a couple of times but nothing else. Constantine confided in Angel that he was a virgin and waiting for that right girl to be with his first time.

One day at the beach they started to talk about their families. Angel confided in him about not having her real dad around and how Leon was so mean to her mom. While lighting up a joint, he became teary-eyed when he explained how his mother wasn't around and how his father was raising him.

"My Dad is never around, and when he is around all he wants to do is party with us. He smokes with us until he passes out from the pot and booze. Now, can we change the subject before I go off and freak out?"

Constantine grabbed her hand and held it for awhile. They started to talk about Kinsey and Monroe and how they really like one another.

"Monroe told me that he and Kinsey had already had sex ten times and they did it the very first night they met. Remember how they took a walk; they did it in the bushes." Constantine said.

"I could never be that slutty! That's so gross," Angel said.

"Monroe does it to anything that has a pussy and will hold still long enough," Constantine said.

They started to walk back to Angel's house and Constantine stopped to give her a kiss.

When she got home she tried to talk with Kinsey, but she wouldn't talk about Monroe at all. She just ignored her. Angel wanted to explain to her how she wasn't the first girl that Monroe had slept with and that she doesn't have to sleep with a boy to get noticed because she was smart, nice, intelligent, and beautiful. Kinsey didn't seem to care that Monroe was probably using her. Angel never brought up her thoughts about the situation again.

That summer was the best-Angel finally found out that not all boys liked her just for sex, and she didn't have to do things with them to get noticed.

Her First Girl And Boy

During that summer Angel started hanging out with Tara, she was a girl who lived directly across the street. Angel was fascinated by the relationship between Tara and her mother; they seemed to be best friends. She watched them as they sat on their porch they laughed, joked, and drank together.

After hanging out with Tara for only a few weeks, it seemed like they had a lot in common. Tara was only a few months older than Angel, yet she seemed to be years ahead of her. One weekend Tara asked Angel to spend the night at her house.

"Well I don't see why not," Angel answered.

"There is a lot that I need to show you Angel, and I can't do it with all the adults around," Tara explained.

That night as she brought Angel into her bedroom, her mom followed them and reminded them that they would have to keep it down if they wanted to stay up late; she had to work in the morning. So far Angel thought that everything was normal, seeing as her mom sounded like a regular mom.

Tara had a tent in the corner of her bedroom. She said it was a place for her to get away from her mom and her mom's friends. After an hour or two, they ended up in the tent, and Angel felt a need to cuddle up to Tara just like she did with all of her other girlfriends. None of the girls thought twice about putting their legs on one another or their heads on each other's stomach to sleep. As Angel laid there and looked at Tara, she was mesmerized by how beautiful she was. Tara's blonde hair, blue eyes, and gorgeous smile had Angel speechless. Tara moved around and put her head on Angel's stomach and she pulled Angel's shirt up a little because she said it was scratching the back of her neck.   They talked about nothing for hours.

"Angel, do you have to leave? Can't you stay with me forever?" Angel looked up to see that it was now morning.

"Christ Tara, you act like we are a couple or something. I can stay but only for a bit," Angel replied.

Before Angel could say anything else she felt Tara's hands on her cheeks and then Tara kissed her. Angel never thought that girls' lips could be so soft, and she somehow wanted to feel more. Tara guided Angels hand up her nightgown and onto her breast. Angel couldn't stop; she felt her hand start to fondle Tara's breast as if it weren't her own hand. Then she moved her hand down Tara's stomach and felt as her stomach started to quiver. She started to rethink what she was about to do, but Tara grabbed her hand and placed it into her underwear. Angel felt this was so different then the things that she did with boys; this felt safe and natural to her.

"Please don't stop Angel," Tara held her close and whispered into her ear, "Don't worry, I won't tell anyone."

They looked up when they heard a voice behind them. It was Tara's mother. She had been watching them, but they didn't know for how long.

"What the hell are you two doing? Get the hell out of there!" she yelled.

They jumped up and went into the kitchen where "B", Tara's mom, was sitting at the kitchen table. Angel felt the cold of the steel table as she bowed her head and knew that she never wanted to bring the incident up again.

B asked them if they were a couple of lesbos. Angel didn't recall ever hearing that word, so she didn't know what it meant. However, from the tone of B's voice when she said it Angel didn't think it was anything good.

"No" they both answered.

"Do you two know what people would call you girls if they knew what you two did?" she asked. "They would call you dykes," she said, answering her own question.

Again Angel had no idea what that word meant either, but by the sound of it, it was something dirty. She was confused. How could something that felt so right to her, sound so dirty and wrong? Tara and Angel remained friends, but they never again talked about what happened in that tent. That didn't stop Angel from thinking about it all the time.

There was a new girl that moved up the street from Angel; her name was Francis. Angel noticed her as she walked up the hill. Francis was sweating as she carried the boxes into her hallway and up the stairs to her apartment. She looked exactly and dressed exactly like the girl "Baby" from "Dirty Dancing".

Angel didn't take long to introduce herself in hopes that this would be another girl for the club. Once Angel introduced Frances to the rest of the crew, they talked about it and decided that she couldn't join the club. They said that she was too stuck up.

Angel didn't care that Francis wasn't part of the crew and hung out with her anyway. She even spent some nights at her house while her mother went to bingo. Francis started to ask if she could spend the night at Angel's house since she hated to stay by herself. She was the first one to notice that there was something different about Leon.

"Angel, he looks at you in a weird way, and he's so mean," she said.

"That's just his way; he's alright," Angel commented.

"He gives me the freakin' creeps the way he looks at you. Are you sure nothin's goin on? You know what I mean," she asked with a wink.

"Oh don't be gross, of course not, just drop it. OK?" Angel asked.

As they watched "Dirty Dancing" one night Fran wanted to dance. She pulled Angel up from the floor and dragged her corner to corner. After only a few minutes, Fran fell to the ground holding her chest, trying to catch her breath. Angel yelled for Fran's mother, and as she did this Fran asked her to leave. Confused, and hurt, Angel walked back to her house. She thought that she knew her new friend, now she wasn't sure.

The next day she found out from Fran what happened to her was common. She explained she needed to take things slower than other kids because when she was just a little girl she had open heart surgery. Angel was frightened when Fran showed her the scar that ran all the way down the middle of her chest. This subject, like Leon, was never brought up again.

Robert came over once a week while Constantine and Miller were over all the time. They all told Angel how beautiful she was and how they wanted her. But, after the experience that she had with Tara; she started to feel differently toward boys. She knew there were different levels of conformability between them. According to B doing those things to girls was wrong and she mustn't ever do it again. Since that was the only exposure Angel had on the subject, she believed it.

In July Meredith's dad bought her a dirt bike. Leon told Angel that the only reason he did that was because Meredith probably does what he wants her to.

"You would get a bike also, if you did what I wanted you to do," he said.

Leon then brought her to his garage, and like usual, he made her go upstairs to his room and get undressed. He held her down on the bed and raped her; this time so hard that she found it hard to breathe as his body lay heavily on top of her. As his sweat dripped onto her face she could feel vomit rise in her throat and she had to fight to keep it down.

"You're still so tight it feels so good," he yelled as his body thrashed on top of her.

At one point he was pounding so hard into her that she blacked out. When she came to he wasn't on top of her anymore. She had no idea how long he went for but as she looked down at her body she saw it was soaked with his sweat. She took the blankets and wrapped herself in them.

"I'm going to tell you about those boys you're hanging out with, they only want one thing and that is your pussy," he said.

She knew that wasn't true because Constantine didn't try anything with her, but Leon continued.

"Your pussy is just right now. If you fuck those boys you'll be a loose woman, and no one likes a loose woman. If those boys have big cocks, your pussy will be all worn out, they will stretch you out, and no man will want you after that. No one will want to be with you when you get older." he said.

This made Angel think that maybe if she were loose, Leon might just leave her alone.

After that weekend, Angel found a dirt bike, just like Meredith's sitting in the driveway when she went outside. Leon came out of the house after she did.

"See what happens when you're a good girl," he said.

She took the bike up to Meredith's house. She already knew how to ride it from practicing on Meredith's. Meredith had invited Robert and Alvin to the pits, and they were waiting for them at the top of the hill. They had a great time riding the bikes around. They rode around for hours. Angel loved how it felt to just be a kid-getting dirty and competing with Meredith on the bikes.

Meredith and Alvin were all over each other, so Robert and Angel just rode a round for awhile. After a couple of hours, Robert pulled Angel close to him. He said he wanted her so badly.

"I'm so sorry for treating you the way I did. I love you. No one could love you more-not even Constantine."

"I have another boyfriend now Robert, and you have another girlfriend. It just won't work out."

"Well, have you done anything with him yet?"

"No, he doesn't push me to do anything like you did."

"Well he must be a fag or something. You're so hot anybody can see that. That's why I want you so badly. I love you, and you know you love me."

They finally left, and Angel didn't talk to him for a few days after that.

Lil started noticing that Angel was hanging around with the boys a lot more than the girls; she knew that it was time for a mother daughter sex talk. She sat Angel down on the couch and she held her little girls hand.

"Now that you're getting older boys will want things from you that you might not want, like sex. You are not allowed to date-never mind sex. If I catch you having sex, I will cut the guy's dick off and hand it to him," she said calmly.

That was their sex talk. Angel reassured her that she hadn't had sex yet and that she and the boys were just friends.

That same weekend Claudia asked Angel if she wanted to go to the movies with her and her friend Jay. As Claudia and Angel walked downtown to the movie theater, a cute boy walked up to them. It was Jay. Claudia hit Angel's arm as she introduced them and said isn't he so cute. Then she told Angel that he saw a picture of her and had wanted to meet her.

They walked into the movie theater and Jay sat beside her. Claudia put her feet up on the back of the chair in front of them. Angel noticed that her boots had silver caps on the end of them, and as she thought to herself that they were very cool, she felt Jay's hand on her knee. Then someone walked up behind them.

"What the hell do you think you're doing with my daughter?" Lil asked.

"Nothing ma' am, we just met today" he answered as his voice trembled.

Lil lifted him out of his chair by his shirt and slapped him across the head. Then she pulled Angel up and kicked her in the butt all the way down the stairs and all the way home.

Angel ran into the house from embarrassment and into her room. As she lay with her face buried in her pillow the door opened and Lil stepped in. She let her know that Audrey was the one that informed her that Angel and Claudia be at the movies with a boy. Angel started to cry and couldn't stop; Lil sat beside her and asked her if she thought that she was old enough to date boys. Lil had no clue that Angel was already dating Constantine.

"I know that I am mature enough to date," Angel answered.

"Ok, you can date since all your friends are, but you can't do anything with these boys, and you know what I mean," she said.

Angel called Jay up and asked him if he wanted to go someplace with her, so they could get to know one another as friends and maybe something more someday. It didn't take him long to answer her.

"No way! Your mother is crazy, and so are you. Just stay away from me!" he said.

One night Leon offered to give Claudia and Angel a ride to the mall. On the way there Leon had an idea.

"Hey girls, I have a trailer not being used and if you guys want to you can have a little party there," he said.

"Yeah let's do it!" Claudia said right away.

So Leon brought them to the store and bought them some wine coolers and beer.

"Leon said we can have some boys there, and he won't tell your mom or mine. He will pick them up later on for us," Claudia whispered in her ear.

"Claudia, if you'll pick the place up, Angel will go with me to pick up the other people," Leon said as he dropped her off at the trailer. He then turned to Angel.

"Remember, no doing things with these boys, or I will tell your mother they were here," he said as he pulled her closer and wrenched his hand up her thigh.

They went to get Audrey, and her mom said they had to bring Marcia just in case they wanted to have a party since Marcia would tell her everything that went on. It was sad but true; she always squealed on them. Marcia was not only the lookout for the club, but she was also the lookout for the neighborhood parents.

Constantine was outside of Angel's house already looking for her. She asked him if he wanted to go to the trailer with her, and he jumped into the truck. Claudia told Leon where to pick up her boyfriend John. John was tall and looked like he must have been at least 21 or so.

When they all got back to the trailer Marcia started looking through all of the cupboards and drawers, and came out with something in her hand. She asked everyone what it was. Nobody wanted to tell her that it was a vibrator, so they told her that it was a hot dog warmer. Everyone else thought it was so funny, but Angel was embarrassed knowing it was Leon's. He probably used it on those girlfriends that her mom would always find out about. They never could tell if Marcia believed them or not because they were always telling her a bunch of horseshit.

Later that night when the sun went down, and the neighborhood of trailers made the woods smell like a cluster of bonfires, John and Constantine pulled out some pot. They all got high while Marcia was sleeping. They felt numb as they consumed all of the alcohol. Angel watched as one by one everyone staggered inside to go to bed.

"Angel do you want to go inside? It's getting a bit chilly out," Constantine asked as his hand came out to greet hers.

"I guess but no funny business ok. I think I'm fucked up since I can't feel my legs anymore," she said as she agreed to go with him.

"Angel no funny business, I promise. I just want to know if you love me because this would be a great time for us to make love-no adults around-you know what I mean?" He kissed her lips softly.

"No way Constantine! I'm not ready for that!" Angel blurted out.

He grabbed her hand and with his other hand he rubbed her cheek.

"I love you Angel, and I can't stop thinking of you. I've never loved anyone this much," he said.

Angel kissed him and told him that she loved him too. He started to undress her while kissing her stomach and her breast. Then he kissed his way back up her neck. It seemed to Angel that his kisses lasted forever. She undressed him, and then there they were both laying there naked, and he just kept looking at her and telling her how beautiful her body was. His skin felt so smooth to her. It was nothing like Leon's rough skin. While Constantine laid on her, all she could think of was Leon but as she turned over and laid on top of him the thoughts of Leon slowly went away.

Angel could tell that Constantine had never done this before. He was shaking when he entered her body; she never stopped looking at him-not even for a moment. She was afraid if she closed her eyes when they opened up it would be Leon doing all of it. Constantine kept asking her if it hurt. He promised he would stop if it did.

"I don't want to do anything you don't want me to" he said.

His arms were wrapped around her tightly as they kissed and made love. Her eyes started to tear up, and he noticed that she was crying.

"It's just that I'm so happy, my first time was with someone I love so much," she said.

"Me to," he whispered.

After they were all done, all she could think about was how mad Leon was going to be at her because of this-what he would do to her if he were to find out. Angel was so mad at herself because she knew the first time should stay feeling special to her, but no it had to be ruined by the thought of Leon once again.

The next day Leon came and picked all of them up. He dropped the boys off in the middle of downtown and then brought all of the girls home. He didn't say anything to Angel all day.

Angel couldn't wait to talk to Claudia and Audrey that night without Marcia around. She wanted to tell them about what she and Constantine did. They all went to Claudia and Audrey's attic. They went there often because no one else ever went up there; it was only them. The attic was dusty smelled like dirty feet and u never knew what creature found its way in, but it was there special hide out. They sat in a mini circle. Claudia went first.

"John and I did it in 22 different positions one for every year since he was born; After all, it was his birthday you know."

"It must have hurt," Angel said.

Audrey looked disgusted. She never even went near boys like that. Claudia told them it didn't hurt because John put ice down there when it hurt and that numbed it.

"Constantine and I made love all night I know now what love really is," Angel said.

Cool the girls approved of that and Audrey thought it sounded sweet.

A week later all of them were downtown, and Angel called home, and Leon answered.

"Angel, how dare you fuck Constantine in my trailer!" he said.

"Leon, I didn't do that," she answered.

She froze as she listened to Constantine's and her voice over the phone moaning and telling each other how much they love one another. Then Leon came back on the phone.

"How do you explain that?" he said.

"How can you tape us doing that? What kind of pig are you?" she asked.

"Angel you told me that you weren't doing anything with these boys.

How can you lie to me like that?" her mom asked. She had heard it all; she was on the other phone.

Angel was embarrassed but she was pissed more that he recorded them. She stomped all the way home, and when she got home her mom yelled and yelled at her. Angel blocked most of it out, but she did hear the part that she was grounded for a long time. The very next day she cried her way out of being grounded.

"Just get the fuck out!" Lil yelled.

"Thank you mom, I love you," Angel yelled back.

"Be home by ten, and don't let Leon see you out of this house, or you will be in a lot of trouble," she said.

Angel left and Constantine met her downtown. They walked to the beach. She told him what Leon did; his only response was he thought Leon must be a pedophile or something. He didn't know how right he was, but Angel did. She said nothing. If she agreed with him he would know her secret, and that could never happen.

The Big Fight

The next day Leon asked Angel to go with him to an auction. Angel didn't argue because she knew that he was still mad about Constantine. He went to these auctions to buy and sell cars. Lil needed a new car, one that would allow her to stop at stop lights and not stall. He always said he wouldn't spend more than $500.00 on a car for Lil because she can walk to the places that she needed to go. Angel was hurt by this because she knew that he wouldn't walk any further than from his truck into the house.

On the way there he mentioned Constantine.

"I told you not to do anything with that boy didn't I? Do you think that I couldn't get rid of those boys for good?" he said.

"I know you can do whatever you want to do," Angel answered.

"Now your pussy is no good, it's used," he said.

"I guess you will leave me alone than" she replied.

Angel just looked out the window hoping that by her ignoring him the discussion would end.

After an hour and a half they were finally there, but Angel stayed in the truck. Angel stayed in that truck for hours. She watched as the sun set and wished that he would have never came back-she could hitch a ride from someone else.

On the way home they stopped at a store to get something to drink. Leon told Angel to go to the bathroom because they weren't stopping again. As she walked back towards the truck she noticed Leon's arms were moving up and down. She wondered what he was doing. As she got into the truck, she noticed her drink had been moved and when she picked it up, she noticed that he had taken a drink from it. She was angry because she never shared her drinks with anyone, but she was so thirsty, she guzzled it

46

down anyway. Within minutes her eyes became very heavy, and then the rest of her body felt like a ton of bricks. She watched Leon eye her as her body began swaying with every corner the truck made. She didn't want to fall asleep. She was afraid of what might happen, but she couldn't keep her eyes open any longer.

When Angel finally woke up, she was in a small cabin out in the middle of nowhere. All the curtains were up and all that she could see were miles and miles of trees. As her eyes focused on her surroundings, she began to feel cold and noticed that she was naked and there was blood all underneath her. She pulled herself up with the help of the homemade wooden frame of the bed causing splitters in both hands.

"Did I start my period? Why am I naked? How did I get here?" The questions circled in her mind. But, the biggest question was where was Leon and where did the night go?

She tried to focus her thoughts as she watched the sunlight stream through the windows. Maybe it was just a nightmare. Maybe she was in hell and would spend eternity on her back on a bed. As quickly as those thoughts flowed through her consciousness, they dissipated with Leon's sudden appearance from the bathroom. As he stood in the doorway, Angel noticed he was wet-like he'd just taken a shower.

"Look at that mess you made; I told you that your pussy would be ruined by that other boy," he said.

"What did you do to me? Why can't I move? That boy didn't ruin me, you did!" she yelled back. "He loves me, and you're the sick pig that recorded us doing it!" she said.

Her body began to shake waiting for his response. He got on top of her.

"I was just trying to protect you, you selfish little bitch! I didn't try to record you, I keep that there for robbers. You can't move because I thought you looked sick, and I put something in your drink to make you feel better-I know how you can't swallow pills. Now get the fuck up and go clean yourself up," he said while climbing off of her.

"I can't get up, and I'm not going with you anywhere," she said hoping that he would leave her there.

"Well no one knows where you are. Your mom thinks the auction was in Maine so she won't know where you are. We're miles away from anyone else, so go ahead and stay here. Nobody will ever be able to find you," he said.

Her hand reached for the side of the bed trying to pull the rest of her body up, and she staggered to the bathroom. She watched in fear as the blood trickled down her legs. She cried as she wiped it up with a soft cloth. Her privates hurt so badly, even the slightest touch made her wince. As her arm slowly reached out for a clean towel, she felt the warmth of her blood as it continued to flow down her legs. She placed a washcloth in her underwear and hoped the bleeding would stop.

Leon placed a blindfold over her eyes as they drove home. He made her lay down on the seat to make sure no one saw her. When they finally reached home Lil was sitting on the couch and told Angel that she looked tired. She ordered her to go to bed.

When Angel woke up she checked to see if the bleeding had stopped. It had, but it still hurt to go to the bathroom. She wanted to see what Leon had done to her, so she took a mirror and spread her legs apart. There were little cuts all over the inside of her pussy lips, as if someone had taken a razor blade to her down there. She had to wear skirts for days afterwards because it hurt to put any underwear or pants on.

Lil sat Angel down one night and asked her if Leon had touched her again. She wanted so badly to say yes, but she thought about it for a minute and said no. If she said yes then her mother would take her and leave, and she knew there was no guarantee they would stay away. When they returned they would face Leon's intense anger, and Angel did not want to go through that again.

"No Mom he has been really nice to me and lets me work with him for a little bit of extra cash" she answered.

"Ok. I just want you to tell me if he does touch you again, and if he does we will leave and never come back," she said.

Days went by and Angel stayed in the house. Then one day Meredith told her that there was a club opening up downtown, and they made plans to go. With the hush money Leon had given her she and Meredith went shopping for clothes.

Angel found a ruffled lace skirt that hit her feet and covered it with a straight jean skirt that was long but still showed the lace. She also wore lace gloves that made her feel like a rock star and Meredith wore almost the same contraption.

Meredith had invited Alvin and Robert to go with them to the club. As the four of them walked down the street, they noticed all the run down houses. They felt they were too good for the neighborhood because of the way they were dressed. They gathered behind the inn downtown and smoked some dope before going inside the club.

It seemed they danced and danced all night. About seven guys danced with Angel. They told her that she really knew how to shake her ass. Everyone said she was a great dancer, and as she danced she felt like a celebrity.

A woman came up to Angel and told her that her mom had called and said that she was not to go outside until the dance was over and to make sure she behaved herself. Angel was embarrassed that her mom was checking up on her. She walked off the stage in shame. She wanted the floor to open up and swallow her.

On the way home Robert held her hand. As they neared her house Angel looked up and noticed Constantine was standing outside by the front door. He saw her holding Robert's hand; he just stood there for a minute, and then started to walk up the hill.

"Nothing happened Constantine! I still love-you please come back!" she yelled.

He came back down the hill. Without saying anything Robert walked over to him and punched him in the mouth then walked away.

"Have her; she's nothing but a tease anyway!" Robert yelled.

"So you haven't done anything with him?" Constantine asked.

"No, I told you that you are the only one I've ever slept with and that I love you," she answered.

Lincoln Middle School

Summer was almost over and soon Angel would be going to a new school Lincoln, Middle School. She had a lot of friends that would be starting school with her, but just like every other twelve-year-old, she was nervous. She knew that she just barely passed the fifth grade and sixth grade would be much harder.

She had to wake up earlier for Middle School than she did for Elementary School. The night before school she got no sleep-thanks to another of Leon's late night visits. The next morning she stood in front on the mirror for an hour teasing her hair. She made sure that every spike was in the right spot. She caked the makeup on making sure that it would be the same for hours.

Francis had agreed to walk to school with her. The rest of the kids lived a house or further away, so they were able to take the bus. Francis had always thought she was way to cool too take the bus. Lil was outside watching them leave for school.

"Angel, come back here right now," she yelled.

Angel walked back up the street where her mom was standing; Lil had tears in her eyes and put her arms around Angel to give her a hug.

"You forgot to give me a hug, or are you to big for that now that you're in middle school?" she asked and put her arms around Francis and Angel and gave them a big hug.

"Mom doesn't cry, I'm just going to school, you're embarrassing me, I love you, and I'll be home soon," she said.

As Angel looked at the living room window, she noticed Summer was looking out-screaming and banging her hands on the glass. Angel waved and blew her a kiss. She blew a kiss back to her, and Angel caught it. Lil took about ten pictures of them walking down the street. It felt almost like she was taking the pictures of them because she would never see them again.

When they finally arrived at school, Angel noticed everyone was standing outside waiting to go in. Meredith had gotten a ride from Alvin and Robert who were both in High School. Angel tried to wave to Robert, but he just turned his head and acted like he was talking to Alvin.

Angel left school happy. The first day was nothing like she had expected. She met so many new people.

They had to go to different rooms for each class and had a different teacher for each subject. Angel's home room teacher was Mr. Graham. He was also a Lincoln Police Officer. This fact scared most of the kids, but Angel thought it was cool. Her friends Mica, Meredith, Miller and Francis were in the class with her. They decided it would be fresh if they all sat together in the back of the room. Mr. Graham did role call, and when he called Miller's name, Miller stood up and said "Yep the king is here." Angel could see that he hadn't grown up over the summer like the rest of them.

"Angel that's a great name," Mr. Graham said.

"Thanks," Angel said while raising her hand.

When she looked over she noticed Meredith and Mica. She heard them making kissing sounds, as if she was trying to kiss butt.

When school was out they started walking home and Angel noticed Robert and Alvin were there to pick up Meredith.

"Angel wants a ride home? I'm really sorry for being an asshole. Can we please be friends again?" Robert asked as he pulled her into the car and put his hand on her knee.

"Yeah I guess, but you don't have to apologize for being an asshole that's just you," she answered with a giggle.

On the way home Robert kept telling her that he still loved her and she needed to dump Constantine, but Angel knew she couldn't do it because she loved Constantine. Robert grabbed her hand then kissed her. She didn't stop him like she should've since she had mixed thoughts on how she felt about him anymore. Angel wondered why she couldn't stop men from taking advantage of her. When they arrived at her house, she walked in, and Summer jumped up onto her.

"I missed you so much Sissy, please don't go no more," she said.

"I missed you too, but Sissy has to go to school," Angel said.

It was times like those that life seemed almost normal. Summer had the ability to do that and Angel loved her for it because for just a minute

Angel could pretend that her life was just like everyone else's. Sometimes Constantine could also make her feel like she was the same as every other girl. But Angel knew that she wasn't normal, and every time she pretended to be Leon reminded her that she wasn't with one of his nightly calls.

The very next day Angel told Constantine that she still loved Robert, and they would have to break up. Constantine cried and told her that Robert will treat her like shit again, and when he did she'd come running back to him. In her heart she knew he was probably right.

Just as Constantine left, Robert showed up and asked her to go to his house, and she told him she just had to tell her mom. Lil just looked at Robert and gave him the evil eye, as if he was to touch her daughter he would, in fact, lose his cock. They walked to his house, and they went to his bedroom just to talk or so, Angel thought. Hours had gone by when Robert suddenly grabbed her hand and put it on his leg. They started to kiss; Angel thought about how good of a kisser he was.

"I know you have been fucking Constantine all summer, but I want to make love to you, not just fuck," he said.

Maybe he's right she thought and continued to kiss him. When they fucked it didn't feel like the love making she did with Constantine. She stopped a couple of times and tried to tell herself that this wasn't right; she was too young. But she knew that wasn't the reason for her lack of passion. She knew that boys weren't for her no matter how good a kisser they were. She always felt uncomfortable doing things with them in the end.

The sex with Robert was really painful because he had a much bigger penis than Leon or Constantine. She wanted him to stop, but she knew he had a bad temper like Leon's. She didn't know what he would do if she were to stop him, so she suffered in silence until it was over. As she walked home she felt her vagina burned with every step she took. Her thoughts turned to Robert and Constantine. She came to the realization that the only reason she let Robert fuck her was because she was afraid of his temper and it was fucking-not making love. Robert was only concerned with his own need unlike Constantine who cared about her. When she reached the house she noticed Leon's truck was there. Going into the house she found her Mom and Summer were gone.

"Come here Angel, we need to talk," he yelled from her mom's room.

"No, not right now. I have to do my homework for tomorrow," she answered.

"Don't you say no to me? Get your ass in here!" he yelled.

He came out of her mom's bedroom and went and locked the front door. All she could think of was that she couldn't let him do anything to her because she was still sore. He came over to her and pushed her face first into the couch. He pulled her pants and underwear down at the same time. He placed his hands on each side of her vagina and spread it wide open.

"Who have you been fucking today, your pussy is all raw," he said as he put his face in between her legs to examine her pussy.

"No one. I haven't done anything with anybody since Constantine and the camper where you taped us," she answered trying to put her legs together.

Within seconds she could feel his penis entering her hard. It burned and felt like her insides were ripping apart.

"Have you started your period yet," he asked.

"No not yet," she cried.

With a hard thrust of his body into hers, he finished inside her. They pulled up their pants and he went into the bathroom to clean up.

"Angel, come here please," he said.

As she walked slowly to the bathroom she prayed that he wouldn't do anything else because she was already torn apart. She stood outside of the bathroom locking her eyes onto the flowered wall paper making sure she didn't look at him because she didn't want him to see her cry.

"I know you have been fucking more and more people because your pussy is all stretched out," he said.

She put her head down and tried to hold back the tears, but they started to fall down her cheeks. She hated when she cried in front of him, it showed her weakness and let him know that he still got to her.

"No, it's been you that has been stretching me out," she replied.

"Well I already told you that if you fuck other men then you are worthless, you're loose, and no one will want you," he said.

"Can I please go and wash up," she begged.

"No, I'm not done with you. You don't seem to care that you are getting all stretched out. Come in here, take your cloths off, and get into the shower. I will help you wash that fucking no good pussy out," he yelled.

"No, it hurts already. I don't want you to do anything else, please," she continued to beg him.

"Haven't you learned by now what happens if you say no to me? Now get the fuck in that shower!" He pulled her into the bathroom and shoved her into the shower.

She did what he said: took her clothes off and stood facing the corner of the shower. He pushed her head into the corner, bent her over, and turned on the shower. The water was hot and splashed her in the face making it hard to breathe.

"Your not wet enough," he said turning the shower on even harder.

He put two fingers in her, and it hurt so badly because of what he had already done. However, that wasn't enough for him, so he put two more fingers in her. She grabbed her own legs trying to hurt them so that she wouldn't think about the pain he was causing her.

"Oh, I'm going to stretch you out so bad that you will know what it will feel like every time you fuck one of those boys. If any one is going to make your pussy bigger it will be me," he said putting his thumb in her along with all his fingers. He now had his whole hand in her. She cried and tried to block the pain but she couldn't. She screamed as he pushed his hand in and out, harder and harder.

"Please stop," she cried.

"I will stop when I'm damn good and ready to stop," he said taking his hand out.

She thanked god that he was done. She was sure that her begging worked that time. In minutes she realized it hadn't he was just getting started. He made a fist and punched her vagina making his whole fist go up into her. She felt her vagina close around his wrist. It was almost like he was trying to punch his way to her rib cage.

"Now, how is that for ruining your pussy? Now maybe you won't make such a big deal out of me just fucking you with my cock," he said.

Angel couldn't move. She just held onto her legs and cried while he pushed his fist in over and over again, she then watched as blood ran down her legs.

All night long Angel laid in her bed and thought of different ways to stop Leon, like she often did. She looked at the clock. It was 3:00 in the morning and she had to get up for school soon, so she finally settled on a plan. She would fuck Robert and Constantine everyday or as many times as she could, that way Leon wouldn't want her anymore because like he said, she would be loose and no good. She finally fell asleep with this brilliant idea in her head. There was no other way to stop him. This would have to work.

Her Mission

The next morning things went as normal as they could go Lil gave Angel a kiss and told her to come right home after school and do her homework. Angel had much more than homework on her mind though. She now had a mission. A mission that had to work, one that would save her from Leon.

"I can't come right home mom; I already have a project that I need to work on at the library. I'll be home around six," she said.

She hated to lie to her Mom, but in her mind there was no other way-no way out of the hell that she was living.

Alvin and Robert picked Meredith and Angel up right after school, and they all went back to Robert's house. Alvin and Meredith stayed downstairs while Robert and Angel went to his room. Angel sat on the bed and explained to him that things were going to change. She explained that she no longer wanted to play hard to get.

"I love you Robert, and I want you," she said.

She got on her knees and unbuttoned and unzipped his pants. He held her head up and assured her that she didn't have to do it. What he didn't know was that he had nothing to do with it.

"I wouldn't be here if I didn't want to do it," she answered.

Her vagina still hurt from the day and night before, so she would have to do other things to Robert to prove to him that she wanted it. She gave him a blow job but had forgotten how uncomfortable having something like that in her mouth had been. She kept her eyes open and watched as Robert moaned with pleasure, trying to keep Leon from her mind. Robert then stood her up and took her pants off. Then he told her he wanted more of her. She pushed him on the bed and laid on top of him. She put his penis inside of her, and it started to burn, but she kept to her mission. Robert seemed to like it as she held his hands down and fucked him hard. She was in awe when she realized she was in charge. That was something she couldn't feel with Leon; she had to keep doing this her way.

That night Angel went to bed still feeling in charge, yet there was guilt involved too for the way she treated Robert like her pawn. She knew in her heart it was wrong to use him the same way Leon used her.

It went on for months; she would go over to Robert or Constantine's house on a day to day basis and have sex with them. Then at night Leon would come in and climb on top of her. Sometimes she could smell him while she slept. The smell of his sweat as it dripped on her made her nauseas.

She was only in the sixth grade. When other kids were thinking about who's going to be their new friend, she was thinking about how long her pussy would hurt the way it did after having sex. Her school work was put on hold until her life was normal, and during the middle of the school year, she started to skip school and hang out with Robert, Constantine or Meredith at least twice a week.

Sometime in February Angel finally started her period. The first time she ran into the bathroom thinking that she peed herself. Meredith ran after her.

"Angel, what is wrong, did you finally start?" she asked.

"Yes. I have pads with me, but my stomach hurts so bad I don't want to go back to class," Angel said.

"Here are a couple of pills that will take the pain away," she said.

She took the pills without hesitation and went back to class. Her pain was gone and she felt a little numb. Her head felt heavy and the words on the chalkboard seemed to float around as the teacher wrote them. It felt as though she had just smoked a joint. After school when she saw Meredith again, she asked her what she had given her for pills.

"It's called downers; they kill any pain you may have. I get them from Alvin and Robert," she answered.

Walking home Angel noticed that it took her a lot longer to reach her house- almost as if she were walking in slow motion. She also thought of all the things that were going on in her life and wondered if the pills would ease all her pain. She really liked the way the pills made her feel, and she took two more before she went to bed. It was the best sleep she had had in a long time.

The next morning when she woke up, she heard meowing in the living room. Leon had brought a kitten home for Summer. Summer and Angel shared a bed at the time, and the kitten began to sleep on her pillow at night. Sometimes Summer would sleep with Lil, and when Leon came in, he would throw the kitten on the floor right before fucking her.

It was Angel's night during the week to help her Mom cook dinner for Leon. Angel heard Leon yelling at the kitten to get off the couch. Lil and Angel always let the kitten go where ever she wanted to go, so she was used to sleeping on the couch. Angel looked into the living room just as Leon slammed the kitten onto her back on the arm of the couch and threw her to the floor.

"Why get a kitten for us if you're just going to hurt it?" Angel yelled as she ran in and picked the kitten up and ran into her bedroom.

"You have to be hard on animals to make them mind you and gain some respect from them," he yelled.

Angel could hear Lil yelling at Leon from her room. She kept yelling over and over again the same thing.

"You don't do that to the animals to get respect from them! You do that kind of shit to impress yourself and make us think your tuff," she yelled.

Angel held the kitten while it took its last breath and died in her arms. She went outside to bury it. She cried the entire time. The poor kitten was just another victim of Leon's. Two or more days went by during which time she didn't look or talk to Leon and neither did anyone else, not even Summer.

Later that week he came into her room and took Summer and carried her to Lil's room. Angel listened as Leon told Lil that Summer had been calling for her. He said that he didn't think she felt very well knowing Lil would insist that Summer sleep with her.

"I need to go to the garage tonight to get some paper work done. I will be back in the morning," he said.

Angel took a deep breath as the front door slammed shut. He's finally gone she thought- one more night of rest without him. Then the door slammed again and his boots came stomping by her door towards her Mom's room.

"Why don't you run to the store and get her some ginger ale to help her sleep, and I will leave when you come back," he said to Lil.

Angel knew what that meant for her; Summer would be sleeping and her mom would be gone. She held her breath and tried to prepare herself for him.

"Angel are you still upset with me? I'm sorry for your cat, please let me show you how sorry I am," he said.

He turned out her night light and headed towards her bed. He then did his usual thing and took off her panties. For the first time she was brave enough and pushed him off of her. He tried again and again, yet again and again she pushed him off.

"Fine, you want to be a fighting bitch, I will treat you like one. I have been a nice guy so far," he said.

He got up and left the room. She felt like she had accomplished something and turned over to go to sleep. Minutes later she heard her door open, and like sometimes before, she pretended to be asleep in hopes he would leave her alone. It was too quiet to be Leon, it must be Summer coming to bed she thought. She then smelled something really bad and felt something beside her. It was soft and furry, but wet and sticky. She still didn't dare move. Then she felt someone climb into bed next to her.

"Summer is that you? Get that wet thing off the bed," she said.

She then picked up the wet toy and tried to hand it to Summer.

"Hold it and realize this is what will happen to you if you ever push me away again the way you did tonight," Leon whispered.

He then got up and turned on the light. Angel screamed when she looked down and realized she was holding their dead kitten. Leon must have gone and dug it up to prove that if she refused him again she too would be dead. He left the room and slammed the door behind him. All she could do was cry. She carefully wrapped her kitten up and brought it out to the dark back yard. While the small light above the back door shined she buried the kitten a second time. She ran into the bathroom just as her mom came home. Lil must have heard her crying because she came to the bathroom door.

"Angel, are you ok honey, why are you crying?" she asked.

"Mom I just started my period, and I have a lot of cramps: I'll be right out," Angel answered.

How would she convince her Mom that she was still on her period when it only really lasted a day or two? She jumped in the shower to make her mom think that she was washing up. She cradled herself in the corner and cried and tried to wash off the dirt that covered her from Leon making her hold the kitten. She scrubbed till her body was bright red- trying to scrub years off. Then she took some red lipstick and put it on a pad and wet it a little bit. She then threw it in the trash with only a bit of red showing. She went to bed and cried herself to sleep. As she dozed off she thought- he beat her again, in this game that he played.

The next morning Lil came in and told her that she should stay home from school, because she had been up all night crying and in pain. Angel first asked if Leon was there or if he went to work. Lil told her that he wouldn't be back until later that week, so she stayed home and watched TV with Summer all day. Summer asked a couple of times about the kitten, and Angel told her that the kitty had to go with its mommy. She was content with that answer.

Lil was right; Leon didn't come back for two days. She let Angel stay home from school both of those days.

Disappearance Of Reality

Angel spent all of her days with her friends, yet she felt all alone. She started to drink a lot-almost every night-sometimes waking up at her friend's houses and not remembering how she got there. She and Kinsey would wait till her Mom was asleep and sneak out of her bedroom and return at around five in the morning. She hated the way her body felt, but she loved that if she was drunk or high then going home wasn't as much of a problem. Kinsey would pass out and Leon would do things to Angel and she would hardly feel it. Her body was empty and dead already. She laid motionless while he tossed her around. The only thing that still felt pain was her mind, nothing that a pill in the morning wouldn't erase.

Leon started to notice that she was drinking all of the time, and one day he asked her if she would like something that wouldn't make her so sick the next morning. He handed her some pills and a bag of pot.

"Here, if you want to feel like your drunk take one of these," he said.

That weekend she went down to the club with Meredith and Kinsey. The rest of the bunch met them out back. She showed Robert and Alvin what Leon had given her, but she told them that she got it from another friend. Alvin seemed to know exactly what all the pills were.

"These pink ones are uppers and will make you really hyper and happy, these yellow jackets will make you feel numb and tired, and these truck drivers will make you just fucked up. Can I have a couple of them?" he asked.

"I don't care, take some, I have plenty," she answered.

"What will happen to me if I were to mix them together and take them," she asked?

They went inside, and she took two yellow jackets and her body went weak. She instantly felt as though she had drank a twelve pack of beer. Her vision became very blurry, and she couldn't walk straight.

She noticed out of the corner of her eye that Constantine was there. He came over and asked her for a kiss. She couldn't resist. He had become so gorgeous over the summer, and he smelled so good she thought. They walked over to the corner of the video games, and they started to make out. She knew that she still loved him no matter what he did or what she did. It seemed as though everyone had disappeared around them- no one was in sight. He turned her towards the wall and started to kiss the back of her neck.

She tried to say no but when she opened her mouth nothing came out. She stood against the wall-helpless and weak. She knew Constantine wouldn't hurt her, but she knew they weren't alone. They were in a club full of people that she knew. He rubbed his hand up her leg, pushing her undies aside then fingering her gently. As her eyesight became clearer she noticed Robert walking towards them.

"You can have my sloppy seconds Constantine, she's your slut now," Robert said.

Constantine didn't stop. She didn't care about Robert and wasn't afraid of what he thought of her.

When Constantine finished he told her to go wash up, he made a little mess and so did she. As she walked towards the bathroom she began to feel weak. Once she finally reached the bathroom, she went into a stall and sat down. One second she was sweating, and the next she was freezing and had goose bumps. It seemed as though she was in there for hours. When she finally went out she looked at the clock and it had only been five minutes. After that night she made a vow to herself never to touch pills again.

Angel's friends started to see something different and wrong about her. She was sick and pale all the time. They worried about her. They took shifts watching over her, but if they said anything to her, she wouldn't talk to them for days. She knew to stay off the drugs she had to distance herself from the crew as much as possible.

That Sunday she went to church with her Aunt Anne like she did almost every Sunday. Although this time she didn't pop any pills before hand. When the pastor asked if anyone had something to thank the Lord for, she stood up for the first time.

"I want to thank the Lord for giving me a chance to be here on this very day," she said.

Aunt Anne just held her hand, and they sat together crying. Then Anne stood up and started to speak in tongues.

Angel later asked the pastor why if God knew something bad was happening to someone, why wouldn't he stop it from happening. The pastor just tapped her on the shoulder and told her that if she came back next week he would have time to have a private session with her. She never went back the following Sunday. She told Aunt Anne that if a pastor can't make time for someone then he isn't worth talking to.

She went to school that following week and started to regret what she let Constantine do. Before going to her first class she had to calm down. She went to the bathroom and took three downers. It only took a couple minutes before she was calm, and she headed for class.

Angel sat at her desk. The teacher began role call. Angel could see her mouth moving, but she could barely hear the teacher's voice. Her eyes became very heavy. She wanted to raise her hand as her name was called, but her arm wouldn't move. At the end of the class, she woke up when the teacher shook her.

"Angel, if you are that tired go down to the nurse's station, and she will check you out and make sure your not coming down with something."

Angel knew exactly what was wrong with her, and she knew that she couldn't let the nurse look at her. She took the pass anyway and walked towards the bathroom, holding herself up with the help of the lockers while sliding down the hall. She finally reached the bathroom and went to the sink and splashed water in her face. She looked in the mirror and realized she didn't recognize the eyes looking back at her. This woman looking back at her was no longer a girl. Her eyes showed years of abuse and anger and hidden sorrow. Her body had bruises that she didn't remember getting. She finally stood up, raised her chin, and took a couple of uppers.

She walked up the stairs to her next class, and it felt almost as if she was floating. The bell rang for the end of the day and she couldn't remember going to more than one class. She had lost all sense of reality; she was now in her own world, and no one else mattered.

She didn't care anymore what happened to her. She only cared about who wanted her and where she would get more drugs. She didn't dare ask Leon for them, and after awhile she didn't have to he would just hand her a bagful every other week or so. She knew where all the drugs and parties were.

She started to date anyone who paid attention to her. She became really mean to boys, but it seemed the meaner she got the more and more they wanted her. She was only twelve and had a list of boys waiting to fuck her.

One night Leon told her that she looked stressed and handed her a couple of pills that she never saw before. She took them without questioning why he gave them to her, but she found out later on that night. She was lying in bed motionless and watched as he laid on top of her.

"Are you high Angel, what do you say to me for giving you all that I have," he asked?

"Thank you, it really helps me get through school and *you*" she answered.

He started to do things to her, but she couldn't move. She could no longer fight him off.

Trying in school the best way she knew how was hard, but she did pass the sixth grade. Lil tried to leave Leon a few more times after the school year ended. They spent a couple of weeks at friend's houses. Then she would go back, and the hell would start all over again. At one point, the police put them into a family's home for their protection. This time Lil told Angel not to say her name or Summer's when they left the home, that way Leon wouldn't find them. But Leon always did find them.

Angel started to question if he really did own the police. Time and time again Lil would call the police after he had hit her, and when they showed up, they asked if she had any physical proof. When she told them no, they would take Leon outside and talk with him. After awhile the police would leave without Leon, and he'd turn around and menacingly head towards the door where they were waiting.

She Told Again

AGE 13

Right after her thirteenth birthday Angel realized that she was now a teenager. She didn't know how other teenagers felt, but she knew that she felt as though she had already skipped over being a child, skipped over being a teenager, and has gone straight to adulthood. She had never played with dolls or acted carefree like children should, and never got the chance to be a teenager whose only concern was the best fashion or music. Leon had taken that all away from her.

That summer she spent a couple of weeks at her dad's house. This was the only time that she felt like she had to stay sober. She still couldn't be happy because she knew that Denise didn't want her there. Denise didn't want to give up any of her father's attention and resented Angel. Angel had to fight for what little affection she got from her dad. She managed to win a few trips with him at his work; he was a truck driver. During these times she loved her dad so much because he was so different from the dad she saw when Denise was around. Angel found they had so much more in common than she thought they had. She tried to communicate with him during these times, but it was hard because she was still furious at him for not being there for her and her mom.

"Why won't you help me and mom Dad? Don't you still love us? Do you love Colby, Katrina, and Denise more than me? Why do they get everything, and we don't even have any food or clothes?" she would ask him.

"You know Angel; it wasn't my decision to leave your mother. She left me, and now I have to provide for my new family the best way I know how. If you want to know why you don't have everything that you should

64

have you need to ask your mother why." His response came out as cold hearted as it sounded.

He saw the hurt in Angel's eyes. Then he changed the subject to school and Leon. Angel knew she could never tell him the truth because if she did he might fight with Leon and that would only make it worse for them. He might even make her live with him, and as well as that might have sounded at the time, Angel knew if that happened she wouldn't be there to protect Summer.

The one thing Angel cared about more than herself was making sure Leon couldn't get to Summer. She was so small that she would never be able to push him off. So in that respect, her visits with her dad couldn't end soon enough for she feared what her Mom and Summer were going through while she was gone.

School was soon going to start, so her Mom called her Dad and asked for some money for school clothes for Angel. After being on the phone with him only a few minutes, tears started to well up and she slammed the phone down.

"Angel, you call your father and tell him you need some money. He won't listen to me" she demanded.

Angel picked up the phone and dialed.

"Dad, mom really doesn't have any money for clothes, and Summer is also starting school, and Mom needs money for her clothes too," she asked.

"Angel I could send you some, but I have expenses also," he said.

Two weeks went by and Lil told Angel that her Dad did send fifty dollars. Angel knew that fifty dollars wouldn't get much, but it would buy her supplies and one outfit from the Salvation Army for the first day. With the fifteen dollars she had left, she brought Summer downtown to let her pick out an outfit.

They walked into Cherrywebb downtown and looked all around. All the clothes were so expensive. Angel finally found the perfect dress but it was $19.99. She took Summer's hand and asked the woman behind the counter to hold the dress for awhile. She wasn't going to let Summer go to school without a new dress.

She brought Summer home and went to the beach where all her friends were.

"Robert, do you want some uppers?" she asked.

"Yeah, and some downers if you have them," he answered.

"I need money for them this time. I need to buy something today," she said.

"Well, we could take it out in trade," he said slapping her ass.

"No, I need the money," she said.

He handed her a ten and she handed him some pills. It was that easy; she was now a drug dealer. She didn't feel ashamed that she had sold what Leon gave her after all, it got Summer her dress.

It was so easy at thirteen to sell drugs; she did it at school, the roller rink, and at the beach. Leon would supply the drugs every other night or so after having his way with her, and the next day she would take them with her to sell.

After that summer whenever Summer needed new cloths or food, Angel made sure she got them. She brought Summer to the Soda Shop almost everyday to eat, but there still wasn't any food at home. After all, she couldn't let her mom know that she had all this money. She came up with excuse after excuse each time she brought Summer out to eat or bought her new cloths. Angel even bought her friends new cloths to wear to the club. Lil never did question why she had money all the time, but every now and then Meredith would ask her where she was getting all the money; Angel simply told her that she worked for Leon at his garage.

School started and it was so hard, Angel was either sleeping at her desk or so hyper she couldn't sit still. The teachers would tell her she had so much potential, and she was wasting it by not trying hard enough. Her response was that there were more important things going on in her life than getting an education.

She started to date more and more boys outside of school. Guys that she met either at the club or at the rink. There was Richard; he had a car and lots of money. Angel would tell her mom that she was sleeping over a friend's house and go sleep at Richard's house. He never really tried anything sexually with her. He would listen to her problems and tried his best to get her off the drugs, so she would try to stay sober before going to see him which meant she only took one or two pills instead of five or six. She respected him as a true friend, yet she stood by her mission and slept with Robert or Constantine everyday.

Leon continued to bring Angel to his garage like usual. One day, his dad was in the living room part of the garage when they arrived.

"Angel go through the side door and wait for me in my office," he said.

She went in like he told her to, and she heard him tell his dad that he should go take a nap, and he'd wake him up later. Leon then came into his office and told her to take off all her clothes.

"Angel your body is just like the models I see in the magazines; you're growing up just right. You know if you want to be a model, as beautiful as you are, you'd have to start in the nude magazines," he said. Then he told her to take off all her clothes and start posing.

"Angel, don't just stand there, make a pose, bend over and spread your legs," she did this as he pulled out his Polaroid camera from his desk.

She did it without questioning him. She knew that she wasn't going in any magazine, but after saying no to him so many times she had learned her lesson.

"Now spread your pussy lips apart," he said.

"Wait! You're not wet enough; I have to get you wet," he said.

She heard him walk over to his desk and open a drawer. He brought over some Vaseline, and put it all in the inside of her butt. Then he put one finger in her butt hole and took a picture of his finger inside her. He took his finger out and put the camera down. He pulled his pants down and left them around his ankles.

"Angel your pussy is so stretched out from those boys, now I have to find another way of fucking you. Grab your ankles it will only hurt for a minute when I first put it in. If you move away than it will hurt much worse," he said.

She did it; she grabbed her ankles as he put his penis in her butt. She screeched, but was afraid to move, although she wondered if it hurt that bad now, how it could get any worse. She not only felt the pain physically but emotionally. She knew that Leon had beaten her in her mission. He had not only made her ruin her vagina, but he now had a more painful way to hurt her.

"Shut up Angel! My dad is in the next room and will hear you," he said as he finished inside her.

"Get dressed and go out back. I'll meet you there after I wash up," he said.

She took the towel that he threw at her and wiped her butt. She shook as she wiped herself because her butt felt like it was on fire.

She waited for Leon outside. He came out, and they walked into the woods a bit. They stopped when they came to a big rock. She tried to sit on it, but her butt still hurt so badly it was difficult.

"Take off your clothes and sit on the rock. Take my shirt to sit on and spread your legs wide," he said.

"No, its broad daylight out, somebody might see me," Angel said.

He grabbed her shirt and yanked it off; she then took the rest of her clothes off. He picked up the camera and started to take her picture.

"Bend over the rock; let me see that wet ass of yours. I don't have all day. Hurry up," he said.

She knew he was getting mad, so she did as she was told. Her knees rubbed against the rock causing a burning sensation and speckles of blood. She looked off in the distance at the cars driving by. One part of her wished they didn't exist, but the other part of her wished they would see her and come closer so that Leon would have to stop. What little pride she still had for herself was all gone on that very day. They went home, and all she could think about was what he would do with those pictures.

The next day she called Richard and told him to meet her at the Elk's parking lot at exactly eight o'clock. He didn't ask her why; he could tell that she was upset. She packed some clothes, kissed Summer goodbye and told her that she would come and get her soon.

She walked down the street knowing that she may be gone forever but she would make sure that someone got Summer away from him. They drove to Richard's house and he went through the front door and like she had done in the past, she climbed through his bedroom window. Richard's family didn't allow girls to spend the night even though he was eighteen he still had to go by their rules, so she had to sneak in and keep very quiet.

"Angel, I told my parents that I need to work tomorrow, so we will leave in the morning till they go to work then come back after they leave. We will have the house to ourselves," he said.

"Richard, we need to talk. I ran away, and I'm not going back home. I want to stay with you I can't take what Leon's doing to me anymore," she cried as she cuddled up to him.

"What about Leon? What does he do to you?" he asked.

She told him everything. He just hugged her and told her that he would get her help. They heard the front door open; it was two in the morning. Angel heard her mom's voice, and she was asking Richard's mom if she had seen her.

"Get into the closet. Stay there, I will handle everything," Richard said.

She sat in that closet for close to an hour and then the door opened. Lil put her arms out to her.

"Come on Angel, let's go. We need to talk and get home. I was so worried about you," she said.

Angel never saw Richard again after that because she couldn't forgive him for telling her mom that she was there.

"Mom, Leon never stopped touching me. He does it all the time, and when you go back to him, it just gets worse. I can't take it anymore. We need to leave for good," she said.

Lil just burst into tears and pulled Angel next to her and held her hand as she cried and cried. Then she told Angel that they would move, and she would need to say her goodbyes to all of her friends in the morning.

"Please don't say anything to Summer, Angel. Leon isn't there, but we don't want him to know that we are moving again," she said.

For the first time that she could remember she was proud of her mom. For the first time her mom had taken the initiative to leave him-no police, no friends-it was all her idea. For the first time she was leaving Leon to protect Angel and not herself. She knew this would have to be for good.

Another New Home

During the middle of the seventh grade they moved to Milton Massachusetts into an old run down two bedroom apartment. The very moment she walked into the apartment, Angel didn't care what it looked like she was just happy that they were away from him again. She helped unpack their things and it didn't take Angel long before she felt right at home. Every time she walked outside she expected to see his truck, she would walk real slow then take a deep breathe when she noticed there wasn't any truck, only the worst smell ever came from the paper mill that was right behind their new house.

The very next day Lil brought Angel to sign up for school. When Angel walked into the school she knew that she was different. She dressed like an adult compared to the other seventh graders. The boys flipped up the collar of their shirts and had an alligator stitched onto them. The girls wore designer jeans and canvas sneakers, half of them walked on one side of the hallway and the others walked on the other side. There were no fist fights going on, no graffiti on the lockers and no kids making out. She felt like Dorothy must have in the Wizard of Oz movie, she was certainly the outsider and she wasn't sure if she wanted to be on the inside. She walked into her first class and sat beside a girl that looked as though she was as popular as Angel had been back at her old school. A few minutes after introducing herself to the whole class she sat down and the popular girl threw a piece of paper at her feet, she picked it up and it read:

"Hi, what is your name again?"

"Its Angel and yours" she wrote back and threw the letter to her.

"Its Stephanie, I'm having a sleep over tonight do you want to come over you can   meet the crew" she wrote.

"Yeah I'll ask my mom and call you, what is your #" Angel wrote back.

As she was about to give the letter back to her the teacher caught them passing the note and sent them to the principals office.

"Angel I don't know how you all ran your school back home, but I run a very tight ship and this behavior will not be tolerated" Mr. O'Connor said.

"Well I'm very sorry but in our school you would not have been sent to the office just for passing a note. I promise it won't happen again" Angel pleaded.

"Well to assure that it won't happen again you will need to bring this letter home to your mother, she will need to sign it and you will return it tomorrow. Thank you, now go back to your class and please don't let me see you here again anytime soon" he said.

Her first day and she was in trouble already, a letter was sent home with her, and her mom would have to sign it. Angel knew if she saw the letter, she would never let her spend the night at a friend's house. Angel went into the kitchen drawer and found a piece of paper with her moms signature on it, for the first time she forged her moms signature on the letter from school. She had this odd sense of success when she saw the signatures looked exactly alike.

She spent that night at Stephanie's house. They listened to music and talked about boys they had dated. It almost seemed as though she was a normal teenager until one of the girls said that she was a virgin and the rest of the girls agreed. At that moment she realized that she was very different from these girls. When they said they fooled around with boys, they meant kissing and rubbing each other and that's it.

"Tomorrow all of us are going to stay after school and have a snowball fight then you can meet my boyfriend he should be there as well" Stephanie said.

"I'm all for that, I'll be there" Angel agreed.

She walked to school with Stephanie and all of her new friends. At school it didn't take long for her to realize that Stephanie was in fact very popular. Now because she was hanging out with her she too became popular in only a day. Classes seemed so much easier than the ones at her last school. In math they were just learning long division, which she had learned in the fifth grade.

She stayed after school and had a snowball fight with all of her newfound friends. Stephanie's boyfriend didn't show up while they were at the school. When it was time for Angel to go home this boy was walking in her direction and asked her if he could walk with her the rest of the way home. As they began to walk he grabbed her hand and told her to please stop. She stood in front of him and he kissed her, he then told her that he had never seen a girl that was as beautiful and different as she was. He was cute, but it was only her second week in Mass., she didn't want to get caught up in all of the drama just yet.

After that weekend she started noticing people were treating her differently than before. One day as she was walking down the hall Stephanie started running towards her and she pushed her onto the floor.

"You fucked my boyfriend you slut, I thought we were friends!" she yelled.

"Who is your boyfriend, I haven't fucked anyone and were not friends we just started to hang out together" Angel yelled back.

"If William is your boyfriend he is the one who kissed me and I told him to stop because I didn't want all this kind of drama!" Angel yelled.

"Why would William say that he fucked you if he didn't" she asked.

Like always Angel had to answer with the same sarcastic remarks that she always had to do.

"Maybe its just that your so ugly and I'm hot so he saw an opportunity to kiss these delicious lips how could he hold back, this was his way to get away from you so he lied!" she replied.

A crowd started to gather around them, but there weren't any teachers yet so they both jumped up and acted like nothing happened. Everyday after that, Stephanie would have all of her friends pick on Angel, throw things at her in the cafeteria, call her names or trip her as she walked by. She was now known as a scumbag, something that was totally opposite of what she was used to back home. All of these things that they did to her didn't compare to the humiliation she endured during gym class. The school had a pool and during gym the kids would have to swim laps. Angel would get undressed and have to stand in front of ten boys and ten girls in her bathing suit. The boys would all stare at her and the girls would yell put some cloths on that bean pole body of yours!!

School became her new hell. She didn't have any friend's and at home she had one thing to look forward to and that was bringing Summer for walks and playing with her. At home they hit a new low financially, just to do laundry Angel would have to turn in bottles for money. She would try to take all the back roads so no one would see her carrying a garbage bag. The back roads were long and it would take two hours to walk there and it would be dark when she got home.

"Mom I need to look like all the other girls in school, they all have perms and I have long straggly hair. Could you please perm my hair we have that old box of solution in the bathroom, it will only take a little while and my bangs are always in my eyes" Angel said.

"Yeah lets do it you will look beautiful with curly hair, it can't be that hard there are directions on the box" her mom answered.

After an hour of the bad smelling perming solution she noticed that her mom had lost the neutralizing solution that was suppose to go on next. Her mom said that they didn't really need it and then she pulled and yanked the rods out of Angel's hair and then cut her bangs. Angel was anxious to see her new hairdo, as she walked into the bathroom she played with the curls and was upset by how tight they were. She calmed down when her mom explained that the curls would settle down after awhile. She looked in the mirror and cried and started to hit the sink in anger. She now looked so much worse than before, her hair looked like a poodle had died on her head and she didn't have any bangs at all. All that night her mom tried to calm her down and apologized over and over again.

"Angel it will look fine in a couple of days and besides that you don't always have to impress the girls at school you are so much more beautiful than any of them." Lil tried.

It was the middle of the week and Lil called Brad and asked him to send her $5.00 a week, so Angel could go to the bowling alley with the neighbors. Brad refused to send her anything; he even started to ignore the court order of ten dollars each month.

Lil made a lot of friends and they had a lot of family in Massachusetts. Lil's sister Phyllis and her husband Rodney lived nearby. They had three kids Vallerie, William and Brandy. Brandy was around Angels age and Vallerie was the eldest, William was the middle child and he acted as so. Angel mostly hung out with Brandy, but she admired Vallerie as the older sister. Brandy and Angel would follow her around everywhere and sneak into her room when she hung out with her friends. William was the one always trying to get the attention from everyone and when he didn't get it he turned into a really mean boy.

It was a regular Friday night and on Fridays Lil always went over to Phyllis's house to play cards. After dinner while the adults set up for their card game William asked Brandy and Angel to go down to the basement with him, he said he had set up a game room. Brandy kept telling him no, but Angel talked her into going, she wanted to get away from the adults for awhile. They went down and William locked the door behind them to insure that no one would bother them. As he walked towards the girls Angel was weary about how nervous Brandy seemed and she tried to back up, but the table behind them stopped her.

"Take your pants down, both of you" he said.

At first Angel thought he was joking so she started to laugh and Brandy grabbed her hand.

"Don't laugh at him Angel it pisses him off" she said.

"No, I'm not taking my pants off for you are you crazy!" Angel said in a stern tone.

As she looked over towards Brandy she was shocked to see that she had already taken her pants down and was looking towards the floor as if it was wrong to look at him. His face had started to turn red and he walked towards them. Angel had pulled her pants down also, and looked towards the floor not knowing what he was going to do. On that day Angel was raped by her own cousin and Brandy was raped again by her brother. After that day neither Brandy nor Angel brought up what happened in the cellar and Angel stayed clear of William. Years later Angel told her mother of the molestation that happened to her and Brandy. This news got told to Phyllis and of course like most of the adults in the family nothing was done or mentioned about it again. They were just told to try and stay away from him.

Years after that Rodney was arrested for molesting Vallerie, but shortly after going to jail Phyllis bailed him out and the molestation continued, and like all the other family secrets that one as well was thrown into the closet, and there it remains.

As adults Vallerie and Angel stayed in touch and Angel didn't hear from Brandy in at least ten years. Phyllis is taking care of Brandy's son because she tried to suffocate him as an infant. William stayed in touch over the years but in 2002 he stole Phyllis's car and after two years he returned home and claimed to be a born again Christian and now lives with Phyllis and her grandson Norman.

After weeks of not going back to her Aunts house, Angel did hang out at the bowling ally and tried to make friends. One day Stephanie showed up with her boyfriend William. She went over and pinned Angel up against the wall, Angel managed to get away and ran home. The next day when she went to school and sat in the cafeteria, she could feel food hitting the back of her neck. Angel turned around and saw Stephanie and her little crew laughing. She felt at her lowest that day. When she finally got the nerve to go over to the teacher and tell her what the girls were doing. The teacher told her to just find another seat and ignore them; they will stop now that they see you talking to me. Angel sat in another chair; soon they began taunting her again. The teacher just walked by and shook her head. At that moment Angel could see that Stephanie didn't only have friends, but she also was the teacher's pet.

When she walked home she noticed a red truck outside it was one of Leon's trucks. She hesitated going inside, she walked around for about two hours then finally got the nerve up to go and see what he wanted. She wasn't surprised to see him sitting on the couch with Summer on his lap and Lil snuggled up right beside him.

"I'm not staying long Angel I do need to explain a little bit to you, I too was touched as a child, and abused by my stepfather, I believe that is why I did what I did to you.." I'm going home, and tomorrow I'm going to get the help I need so that we can be a family again" he said.

When he left Angel told Lil about what happened to her in school.

"Mom I'm not popular like I was in Lincoln, I get picked on everyday and they treat me like a scumbag" she said.

Lil hugged her and told her that if you have to fight to get respect then you must do what is needed to do. The very next day at school Angel walked in with her head up high, she sat in the same spot in the cafeteria and it didn't take long before they all started in on her.

"Stephanie you are just jealous of me, because your boyfriend knows I am better looking than you are, that's why he kissed me on that day" Angel said.

"Well if you think your all that, why don't you do something about it" she replied.

Angel ran towards her and punched her in the mouth, they fell to the ground hitting and scratching each other for some time. A few teachers came over, and it took two more to drag Angel off of her. Within minutes she was sitting in the principal's office waiting for her mom to get there.

"Angel what happened" Lil asked.

"Mom I told you that I couldn't take getting picked on anymore, I told the teachers plenty of times and they did nothing" Angel answered.

"Did she tell you guys about the kids picking on her and if she did what did you do about the other kids" Lil asked the principal, and the teacher that was there?

"Angel has come to me a few times, but I told her that girls will be girls and it takes the bigger one to walk away" she answered.

"It seems like you only want to punish the girls that take up for themselves, that is why this will be Angels last day, we are moving back to Lincoln" she said.

For only a moment Angel was happy, then she realized that this meant, she would see Leon again! They went home and without telling Summer about why they were moving again all of their stuff was already packed. Angel was hurt and discouraged because back at the school she thought her mom wanted to move to protect her but as she looked around she realized that her mom had already planned on going back to Leon. That same night they were back in Lincoln at the same apartment they had left. It seems as though Lil didn't plan on staying away very long, all of their furniture was still there. Like always Leon was standing there waiting for them with open arms and like always it didn't take long before Lil was in his arms again.

The Same Ol' Thing

AGE 14

Angel went back to school and her friends, boyfriends, drugs and parties. It was like she had never left. There was something else that never changed, Leon soon after they returned he was back hitting Lil, calling her names and raping her for hours in their bedroom. He bought Angel a naughty nighty one night and she figured that she would save it and would wear it for Constantine. Leon had something different planned for it.

"Angel come in here please and bring the nighty with you" he said.

"Alright I will be right there, but I will not bring the nighty with me" Angel said.

"Oh you became a sassy girl in Mass. Now get the fuck in here with that naughty nighty or else" he yelled.

Angel took her time hoping that her mom would come home and she wouldn't have to go in and see him.

"Angel I'm not going to do anything to you please come in here" he said.

Angel finally went into the room and he was lying on the bed in nothing but his underwear.

"Please take off your clothes and show me what the nighty looks like on you" he begged.

"Leon you promised all of us you were going to change" she reminded him.

"I'm not going to fuckin touch you I just want to see what you look like in it, now take them cloths off and change!" he yelled.

Angel noticed how mad he was getting and did as he told her to do. She stood there in front of him. She felt humiliated, but also happy that he wasn't touching her.

The door swung open and Angel was in shock as her mom stood there looking at her.

"What in the hell is going on in here!" Lil asked.

"Nothing I am trying on part of my Halloween costume. I didn't even realize that Leon was in here. You have the long mirror so I wanted to see the whole thing" Angel lied pointing to Leon.

"Angel go and get dressed now and no your not wearing that for Halloween" Lil said.

Angel picked up the mail the next day and her report card from Milton was finally there. Angel opened it and was surprised to see that she had gotten three A's, she hasn't received anything above a D for about four years. Angel showed her mom and she gave her a few dollars and told her that she was so proud. When she went to school she tried harder than she ever tried before. She knew that she wouldn't make it on drugs so again she tried to stay clean. She found herself pretending to be high when she was around her crew, if they all knew that she was clean they would pressure her. This only went on for a month or so before Leon started to rape her again. She started the drugs first and then started to sleep with different boys again. She knew that her life was never going to get any better than it was right then.

The school got a new guidance councilor finally a female this time. Angel began to see her once a week as the teachers suggested. She could tell right away that Angel was on drugs and had very low self esteem. They soon developed a strong bond between them. Angel started too confide in her things she never told anyone else. She sometimes couldn't wait to see her she would ask to see her, more than she was suppose to.

"Angel have you ever been forced to do things that you didn't want to do" she asked.

At first Angel contemplated on saying no, then she knew how much she trusted her and could tell her anything and she wouldn't judge her. Angel also thought of how her life was just then and if it could have gotten any worse than she would be dead. The only thing that Leon could do to her that would be worse then the things he has already done would be to kill her. The only reason she was still alive and hasn't killed herself yet was she knew she had to be there for Summer and her mom.

"Do you tell anyone about the things that I tell you in here" Angel asked.

"No sweetie this is just between you and me" she answered.

"Yes my stepfather has been molesting me ever since I was six years old" Angel said as the tears started to come down her cheeks and she could feel her body shaking out of control, shaking from mostly fear and also from relief that now someone else knows.

"I have told my mom over and over again, but then we move and he finds us and she goes back to him, things only get much worse each time" she said.

Angel stayed in that office for three hours that day and told her everything that Leon has done to her. She finally went to her next class and felt as though a whole building had been lifted off her shoulders. She knew that she wouldn't tell anyone but also she now had someone to tell when he does things to her.

Months went by before that building that had been lifted came crashing down. The principal called Angel down to the office, as she walked down she looked out the window and noticed a police car outside. Her body began to stiffen and she thought about running back upstairs and hiding. As she approached the office she nearly fell to the ground when she saw her new friend the councilor and the police officer in the office. In her mind she knew that she must have told the officer the things that she promised would stay between them.

"Angel please come in here and sit down we need to discuss what has been happening to you at home" this police officer said.

"How could you, you promised that you wouldn't tell anyone. I will never trust you again or anyone else for that matter!" Angel said to the councilor.

"Angel I had to because of this thing that your stepfather has been doing to you. I must report any abuse to the police, I'm so sorry" she replied back and turned around and left.

"Angel here are the things that you said happened to you. Can you please read them and tell me if there is any truth to this" the police officer handed Angel a stack of papers.

"No nothing is true that I told her, I said all those things just because I wanted the attention, my stepfather is great to me. I just wanted to get out of class and I did, didn't I" she said back.

"Ok Angel go back to class and I will discuss this with your parents then they can decide on what they want to do" he said.

After that nothing was ever done about the things that Angel had said to that councilor, but she never talked to her again.

That weekend Claudia introduced Angel to her cousin Henry he was older than Angel but he was so cute. They started to date and the sex began to become more and more of a habit for Angel a habit that she couldn't break. Angel also had a couple of girls that she slept with, when she was with them she felt safe she didn't have to be in control and she didn't feel dirty afterwards.

At just thirteen she thought that she had no future, she didn't care about herself and slept with more people than an average adult would sleep with in their whole life time. Her life was spinning out of control and no one was there to stop it.

Her fourteenth birthday was coming up and she had already slept with around twenty different guys. The boys would call her a slut and tell everyone how easy she was but she still thought that she had more friends than anyone else. In her mind she would justify sleeping with them, because they would wear a condom and it was no different than being at home with Leon.

One day Leon had told her that he needed to start wearing condoms so that he wouldn't get her pregnant. She didn't tell him that she had already been on the pill ever since she was twelve to slow her period down. Lil told Angel the next day that Leon might have caught some STD from someone else he slept with. Angel thought to herself this would explain why he wanted to wear a condom all of a sudden. Then she started to notice these bumps on her vagina that she never had before. She decided to question Leon about giving her an STD and of course he denied it. She finally worked up the nerve and called the doctor to make an appointment, because she was afraid of what they would say to her it took her almost a month before she had an opening in her schedule.

Angel walked to that office on a sunny Wednesday and saw everything so different. The trees looked liked they were dying and the cars all went by her so slow, it was almost as if every person that went passed her knew how dirty she was. She walked into the office and forced herself up to the receptionist desk. The women behind the counter looked to be only a few years older than Angel. She became frightened to speak her words clenched to the inside of her mouth.

"Can I help you miss, do you have an appointment today or are you here to make one" the receptionist asked.

Angel looked at her name tag and noticed that her name was Lillian, she froze because this must have been a sign from god telling her that her mom was there watching over her.

"Yes I am here to see the doctor" she finally replied.

"Is this a sick visit or a well one" Lillian asked.

"Well I don't think it could be anymore sick than this" Angel almost slapped herself after that.

"What is your name miss and I will try to get you in as soon as possible" she said.

"My name is Angel and I feel very sick please hurry" Angel ran to her seat and hid her face behind a magazine.

Finally the nurse came out and called her name Angel stood up like a soldier and followed behind hoping that any minute now she would wake up. The hall to the room seemed so long.

She laid on the white paper that was covering the hardest bed she had ever felt. She covered her eyes while the doctor put her legs in stirrups and pulled her flesh open to examine the mess that she had gotten herself into. The doctor told her that she had one of the worse cases of venereal warts he had ever seen and she would have to tell all her partners what she had that way they could be tested. She explained to him that all of them wore condoms. He replied by telling her that you never know if one had ripped or not. She felt ignorant saying anything because she couldn't tell him that Leon had given them to her. The first person she knew that she had to tell was her mom. Angel wasn't sure why she hadn't put two and two together and knew that Leon had given them to her. Lil automatically thought she must have gotten them from Constantine, because this is the only boy she thought she had slept with.

Lil thought that if it weren't Constantine than it had to have come from this older boy Angel had been seeing. He was 22 years old and his name was Bill he lived in Moulton. Bill was a version of Bon Jovi but with huge muscles. Angel met him one night at the club he had told them there he was only 17 and they let him in. The same lie he had told Lil and she to had believed him. He started to pick Angel up on the weekends and she would spend the night at his house while telling her mom that she was spending the night at Meredith's or some other girlfriend's house. He had his own place and at times Angel would pretend to be his wife and make him dinner and clean up after him. When Bill showed up on the day after Angel's wart confession, Lil sat him down and told him what Angel had been diagnosed with, then she waited in the bedroom for him to leave.

"Angel are you in there" Bill asked while knocking on her door.

"Yes, come in if you want to" she said.

They sat on the bed and Bill held her hand, then came closer and hugged her.

"I'm not going to leave you, because of what you have, you are the best thing that has happened to me and I love you" he said.

"Please understand that I have done things in the past that I regret but I am trying to straighten my life out and I love you too, can I please spend the night over your house, I just want to be with you" she asked.

"I will go and ask your mom if you can stay with me I will tell her that you will spend the night on the couch" he said.

Only a few minutes went by and Bill came back into her room and told her that Lil said yes and to pack her things.

They went and picked up Meredith and she went with them because Bill's best friend wanted to meet her now that she and Alvin split up for awhile. When they got to his house Meredith and Bill's friend went into the bedroom to talk that same night she slept with him. While Bill and Angel stayed in his room he told her that he still wants to make love to her and he will make sure to wear a condom. It did hurt a little bit but Angel just loved afterwards when they laid in each others arms for the rest of the night.

That following week Angel had another appointment at the doctors. As she laid there on the table with her legs in stirrups again the doctor decided it would be best to burn the warts off with liquid acid. As they started the process all she could do was hold onto the table and cry from pain and embarrassment. As she walked home she still was in so much pain she would have to stand still in between every three or four steps.

The doctor told her that she couldn't have any intercourse for at least 30 days. This made it very difficult for her, it may sound strange to some people but it was like a bad habit, like cigarettes she now found the need to have sex everyday and the attention from the control she had on these boys that she slept with. Though the thing she hated most was Leon didn't seem to care about the doctors orders, he raped her anyway and sometimes this would open the scabs that she had suffered from the burning. She would bleed for hours afterwards. He raped her so hard that her vagina would be rubbed raw and as she peed the holes from the newly rubbed sores would burn.

The end of school finally arrived and she received her report card and on the bottom it had read that she would be retained in the seventh grade for the following year. This didn't surprise her she knew that she didn't put a lot of effort into her work she was just excited that summer was finally there.

Mom told her to come right home that last day, because she needed to talk with her about something important.

"Angel Leon is fixing up a new house for us and you are going to have another little sister or brother" she said.

"Mom you know that I love Summer but are you sure you want another baby and I don't want a brother I wont love him as much as I love Summer. I don't want to move away from all my friends they are all I have" she said.

"You will love this baby just as much as Summer and you will help Leon fix up the house this is going to be a new beginning for us" she said and the conversation ended.

Angel went into her room and cried herself to sleep, when Lil said a new beginning for all of them, she had no clue what this meant for Angel. She had no friends' houses to escape to and having a house with Leon gave him more control over them.

Angel had to find someone to talk to about this. She couldn't talk to Meredith, because of what Leon said about her father. She wanted to talk with Francis she was the only one that really listened to her and didn't judge anything she did or said. She went to her and cried as she told her everything Francis kissed her forehead and told her she would always be there for her.

Goodbye Francis

Francis and Angel started to hang out more and more after that day. Fran invited herself to spend the night more often at Angel's house. Angel even gave Francis a drawer to keep her clothes and personal items in, however, Fran never asked to hang out with Angel and the crew. At school Angel was ignored by Fran, she stuck with the upper class girls "AKA the snobs" as everyone called them. She started to wear only name brands and would talk to Angel during the classes they had together, even then it seemed like an obligation. She was becoming different from the crowd that lived on the hill, including Angel. Still after school she would go to Angels house or Angel would come to hers. Angel finally had enough and so needed to talk to Fran about the way she was making her feel.

"Francis why do you give all of us the cold shoulder when we see you in the halls at school" Angel asked.

"What do you mean cold shoulder?" she answered.

"Well, when we see you in the hall and you are with "the snobs" you act just like them towards us with your nose in the air. You have to remember where you are from and who your true friends are and it's not them. If u got in trouble you think for one minute they would come to your rescue, fuck no!" Angel said.

"That's the problem, I don't want to remember where I'm from, I hate this hill and I don't want to grow up to be like our mothers, you know; poor and depending on men to get us by" she answered.

Angel knew exactly where she was coming from; she thought by hanging out with an upper class of people she also would be upper class. The crew decided to give Francis some room to let her find out who she really is, and nothing changed during school, she was one of them but after school she was one of the crew.

It seemed to be like any other Tuesday as Angel sat in class surrounded by friends laughing, joking and imitating the teacher before she came into the room when an announcement came over the loud speaker.

"Good morning students, May we have a moment of silence" the principal said.

To my surprise everyone became very silent, not knowing why. The urgency in the principals voice made students pause and listen intently to what he had to say.

"We lost a great student this morning, let us remember Francis and the way she touched all of our hearts" he said with remorse.

Angel looked around and listened to the screams of sorrow from the kids in her class and also from the halls. She sat stunned and the room around her became surreal, it was like a nightmare.

"What is real about a thirteen year old dying" Angel asked the girl next to her.

"Angel maybe you should go home and take some time to relax" Meredith told her as she gave her a hug.

She knew how close Francis and Angel had become.

"Please if any students would like to talk to someone come down to the office" the principle announced.

Half the class stood up and walked out. Angel wanted to talk to Francis' mom and her mom too, she tried to get up but she started to shake all over. When she finally got to her feet, her legs gave out and she fell to the floor. Lying on the floor, she was surprised to see Miller standing above her with his hand extended out to help her up.

"I need to go, I need to get out of here" she said crying.

As she ran to the office the halls became longer and longer. She got to the office and asked the secretary if she could leave. The secretary gave her a dirty look and slammed her pencil on the desk.

"We'll see, what's going on here is a crisis which has happened to a student and everyone wants to go home! Even those who didn't know her, they assume that this is a good time to get a free day off. So, to answer your question whether you can go home or not the answer is no!" she said loud enough for all to hear.

"She was one of my best friends, I need to talk with her mom or my mom, and please let me go home" Angel pleaded again.

"Angel I've never even seen you two walking down the halls together.

I know the crowd she hung out with and I know the crowd you hang out with and they are nothing alike. Now please go back to class" she said.

"I am her best friend and I am leaving, you bitch!" Angel screamed as she walked out the door.

She had never talked to an adult like that before, so she was very nervous walking home. She couldn't even remember walking all the way home, but there she was sitting in her living room telling her mom what had happened. The next thing she knew she was running up the hill to Francis's house, her mom answered the door.

"What happened" Angel asked.

Her mom put her arms around her and brought her into the house.

"The doctor changed her prescription for her heart, it was stronger than the one she had before. I guess it was too strong because her heart failed" she said tearfully.

"I don't understand she was only thirteen, how does a thirteen year olds heart just stop?" she asked.

"She loved you Angel, her wake will be the day after tomorrow, please be there she would have wanted you to say goodbye" she said her voice breaking.

Angel agreed that she would go, never being to a wake or a funeral before she had no idea what to expect. She left and went home and cried for the rest of the day and night. The next day in school Francis was the topic among everyone, the following day she went to the wake. She was standing at the door and became surrounded by kids that she had never met, they all were crying. As she stood in the corner she noticed Francis's mom walking towards her. She tried to think of what she should say, but she couldn't her mind was a blank.

"Angel lets go up honey and say goodbye, I will go with you" said her mom.

"I can't, I don't know what to say" Angel said holding her stomach hoping not to get sick right there in the middle of the service.

"You will once you get up there, I've never known you to run out of words" she said with a smile.

They went up to the coffin and there she was, she looked so peaceful, but it looked nothing like her. They had dressed her in a business woman's suit, makeup caked on her face and her hair slicked back. She always looked care free even her hair was care free, curly and going everywhere. She would have never been caught anywhere in those cloths of that style.

Angel's hands started to shake and she kissed her finger and put it on Francis's lips. That's how they always said hello and good bye.

"Come on sweetie, everyone is waiting to see her" her mom said, while pulling her hand.

She tried to move but she couldn't her feet were frozen to the floor. She took the picture that her mom had taken of them the first day of school out of her pocket and placed it at Francis's side.

"Now we will always be together on that hill and looking as goofy as ever. You got your wish Fran you got out and someday I will too and then we will be together again" Angel whispered making sure her mom didn't hear her.

Months went by and she finally got the courage to go and see Fran's mom. When she opened the door she was shocked to see her mom wearing Francis's clothes. She got a perm put into her hair and she looked like Fran.

"Hello, sweetie I'm glad you are here, I have something to show you, I think she would of wanted you to hear this" she said and went to her room and brought out a diary.

"I don't think we should be reading her diary" Angel said and put it back on the table.

"Well I think there is something that you should hear from her diary" she persisted and began to read from the diary.

"Today I saw Angel in the hall way and she was laughing and having fun with the bunch, she looked so happy and it made me realize that I have been such a bitch lately to them. Well not just lately like most of the school year and now it's almost the New Year. The one thing that I wish I could change and do better for next year would be to change back to my old self, but most of all I need to tell Angel how much I love her, she is like a sister to me. I have been so mean to her and she never changed her attitude towards me" she read from the diary.

"I know that she thought this would have made us closer but for me we were never apart. I loved her like she was my sister too" she said.

Angel still sees her mom from time to time, she has changed over the years and she will stand on the side of the road dancing and waving at cars. Angel listens while teenagers walking by call names like the "crazy dancing lady." She still wears Francis's clothes, and more than fifteen years have gone by since her death.

In everybody's life they should be so lucky to have the privilege that Angel had to know a person like Francis.

The New House

"Angel wake up we need to get ready, Leon is finally bringing us to see our new house" Lil said shaking Angel.

They walked in and Lil began to point out things in the house that she thought had real potential and things that must be thrown away. All Angel could see was trash and wall paper that seemed to be running away from the walls. The place smelled like ammonia and spoiled food. In some corners to her surprise, there really was spoiled food. How could anyone live like this she thought to herself?

"Angel you will have to come out with me sometimes and help fix this house up, now that there will be three of you, you and Summer are much to old to share a room, we will need another room just in case your mom has a boy" Leon said.

Summer and Angel went upstairs to look around and while Summer found the good in everything, Angel found the rooms that she knew would be the places that Leon would rape her in.

"Mom does this mean that I will have to change schools, because I really like my school and I have so many friends there" Angel asked.

"Well when school starts again you can go with Kinsey to her school and check it out before you say you don't want to go there" she answered.

They went back to their house and Angel began to call all of her friends and tell them about her moving and they all said the same thing that her new school had nothing but snobs there. That summer she tried real hard to have fun with her friends and to forget about moving.

One night Leon had brought home a camper and said that Angel could use it to sleep in when her bedroom became too hot and he parked it out back. Kinsey and Angel spent a lot of nights in the camper mostly pretending that it was there apartment. Kinsey invited Monroe over one night and he brought a friend that Angel knew, his name was John. The summer Monroe and Constantine had started this crew "Muscle" and there were more than thirty boys already in it. John was one of the head guys and he drank a lot. That night he had brought some Jack Daniels, Angel had never drank hard stuff before but she was willing to try it. John began to tell her how the other guys said that Kinsey fucked like a jack rabbit, so this told her that Kinsey had slept with more than Monroe. That night became a competition for Angel and Kinsey, Angel had something to prove to John, and she had to prove that she could fuck better than her stepsister. Being drunk Kinsey and Angel didn't care that they were next to each other screwing these guys and they could see one another.

Again the next morning Angel felt so dirty waking up to this guy that she had just officially met the night before. This isn't what made her most upset she knew that Monroe would tell Constantine that she slept with John. The only thing that made her forget about Constantine and what he thought of her was taking a handful of downers and she did just that. She sat on the end of the bed and slowly felt her body fade away from reality. She straightened up her body as she heard her mom yelling her name. Oh my God she thought what if her mom knew that the guys had spent the night. She got up and told the guys to wait for her to go in her house before they left.

"Angel your cousin Claudia and Cynthia was in a bad car accident and Cynthia died." her mom said.

Claudia was her Cousin Patrick's wife and Cynthia was there four year old daughter.

"Mom how about Claudia is she okay" she asked.

"Patrick is up at the hospital now; we will know how Claudia is doing once we get up there. Go and wash that make up off you look like a tramp, now go, hurry up" she said.

Angel ran to the bathroom and looked in the mirror as she washed her face, her eyes were half closed and she looked like hell from the downers. It was ok though she thought because her mom would just think that she had been crying and not high. Everyone met up at the hospital parking lot. No one wanted to go in by themselves and everyone thought that the other person would have more answers than they did. All thirty of them walked into the hospital together and walked slowly towards Patrick who was crunched over the couch in the waiting room. Claudia was in critical condition and only Patrick was aloud in to see her. They all watched as he went in and out of that room to see her. Later on that night Patrick informed the family that Claudia had died also.

Still being high Angel couldn't really let her feelings show. Some of the family asked her if she cared at all about what had just happened, you show no emotion they all said. Her world had already crumbled from under her feet, nothing could make her show emotions to people.

The funeral and wake was going to be the following week and Lil asked Angel if she wanted to go with her. Angel just didn't know if she could go to another funeral after Fran's. Angel went to bed that night and cried as she thought about how much she would miss them and how would her best cousin deal with what happened to his wife and child. Angel couldn't go to the funeral and see them in the casket the same way she saw her best friend just months ago. She wanted to remember them as they were while they were alive. She remembered playing with Cynthia in the sand at the beach and how her smile would light up a room. They were both the kind of family members that you would want to invite to every family gathering. She didn't know what she would say to Patrick when she saw him.

That very next day Leon asked her to go to the new house with him.

"I'm really not in the mood to be around anyone today" she said.

"I didn't ask you if you're in the mood or not you're going to help me today" he said.

They arrived at the new house and they worked on the kitchen floor, she learned how to put a floor together. Leon pulled out his tape measurer and told her to take off her clothes. Angel stood there in the middle of the kitchen naked while he measured her body. Angel felt her arms go up in slow motion while Leon measured her breasts; she looked at the pineapple wall paper fighting to come off the walls.

"Well your measurements are 36", 24", 36; your body is perfect for modeling." he said.

"I decided that I don't want to be a model I'm going to be a hair dresser" she said while covering her breasts.

"You know you're not even smart enough to pass the seventh grade you need to finish school to become a hairdresser. Models only need to take direction and be good looking." he said.

"Alright whatever I want to go home now." she said and she picked up her clothes and began to get dressed.

"You're not going anywhere we need to christen the house, go and lay on the living room floor I already put a rug down for us." he told her.

"What does christen mean?" she asked walking towards the living room.

"I'm going to fuck you; do you need any more explanation" he said.

He raped her right there in the middle of their new living room. The new carpet smell made her stomach turn. She felt the rug dig into her knees as Leon rocked her back in forth while inside her. She stood up and looked at her knees and they looked as though she had just put then over an open flame. Just when she thought they were going home Leon decided to show her where they might have bought a house. They drove for almost an hour and ended up in the middle of the woods on a dirt road.

"Leon I didn't see any houses on this road where are we going." she asked.

"Don't worry we are here, get out" he answered.

There she was naked, on the ground in the middle of nowhere waiting to see what Leon would do to her next. It wasn't long before she found out what he wanted, he sat there looking her up and down, and then proceeded to take off his cloths.

"Turn over now, at least this time no one will hear us, stay like that and don't move" he said sternly.

He took something out of his pants pocket; it was a small tube of something. He lies her on her back and put his wet dirty fingers in her butt. He then continued to put the stuff all over his penis. He spread her legs and put his hard penis in her butt he was a lot rougher than the time at the garage. He was right no one was around to hear her cry, screaming, or say no. She scraped at the dirt under her and tried to think of something else. But all she could think of was how her body felt as he jammed his penis in and out and how it felt like there were needles going inside her.

"Your ass is the only tight hole on you now, so don't be afraid if you see a little blood that's normal it's like losing your virginity again" he said.

"Nothing about this is normal" she screamed.

He got up and left her there; she could have gotten up and ran but where to, for miles around there were only trees. He went to the truck and came back with a paper bag; and she laid there naked waiting for her next punishment from him.

"Spread your legs and close your eyes" he said.

"Please don't make me close my eyes, I promise I won't move I just don't want to close my eyes" she pleaded as he pulled out a silver gun.

"Please don't kill me, Leon I promise I will never stop you from doing what you want to do" she begged while keeping her legs opened making sure not to move and make him angrier. She knew that she couldn't die because if she was gone he would do this same thing to Summer.

"I'm not going to kill you I'm just going to show you that I am able to do whatever the fuck I want to do to you and no one will ever see or hear you" he said and put the same wet stuff that he used on her butt on the end of the gun. Then he bent down and ran the gun up and down her leg.

She turned her head for a moment so she couldn't see what he was going to do next. He then put the end of the barrel of the gun into her vagina; she could feel her flesh ripping as he took it out and then put it back in again. After that day she never questioned how bad it could have gotten, she knew that at any moment while lying on that ground she could have died and no one would have ever known.

The next day she went to Leon and asked him when the house would be ready to move into. Sometime in the middle of the summer before you go into the eighth grade. All that summer Leon had his way with her at the house he told her that this was their house and not to worry about the rest of the family they were the only ones that worked the hardest on it.

That following week Patrick had a get together at his house to remember Claudia and Cynthia. Angel walked around the whole house trying her hardest to avoid Patrick, but finally he caught up to her and put his arms around her.

"Angel you are my favorite niece and I love you, I'm ok with you not going to the funeral and wake. Aunt Lillian told me that you were afraid to go" he said.

"I'm not afraid to go, I just want to remember them the way they were. I'm sorry and I love you too" she said as she squeezed him and walked away.

"It's ok and I know how much you loved them" he said as he grabbed her arm and hugged her tight.

"You know that Little Patrick was in the car with them when they crashed and he's outside playing maybe you can go and show him a friendly face" he said.

Little Patrick was her Cousin Patrick's little boy he belonged to Patrick and his ex girlfriend. He was only six and he was the cutest little boy, he looked a lot like his dad. Angel went outside and played with him and he laughed as she tickled him.

For days that is all anyone talked about, the way they looked in their casket. They buried them together and people said they could see the scar across Cynthia's head from the crash. Nobody mentioned how beautiful they were before and how happy they always had been, but Angel remembered and she has no memory of them in the casket and she liked it that way.

Where Did The Days Go

Angel began to take more drugs and spend more time away from home. She spent most of her time with Kinsey and Meredith; they went to a different party every night it seemed. Meredith and Angel were invited to Alvin's Birthday party and as soon as they walked in she noticed the keg in the corner and headed straight for it avoiding everyone that came over to say hi. Angel began to look around for Robert, but she didn't hear or see him anywhere. Later she heard Alvin tell Meredith not to let Angel go upstairs, if she did she would see something that she might not be able to handle. She knew at the time she would have to go upstairs if she wanted to see Robert and see what he was hiding.

She walked upstairs helping Meredith along the way because she knew at anytime Meredith was going to throw up. She sat in the bathroom holding Meredith's hair back as she threw up, when she heard a noise coming from the bedroom next door. She opened the door where the voice was coming from and was shocked to see Kinsey riding Robert like a jack rabbit. She held back the tears and ran downstairs and asked herself over and over why would either one of them do this to her.

The rest of the night was a blur and when she woke up at three in the morning she found herself naked on the living room floor lying next to her biggest crush Dawson. She looked around for her clothes and couldn't find them, then Dawson handed her his oversized shirt. She got up only to fall again when she noticed that the room was full of people some lying only feet away from her and some sprawled across the couch. Looking around she noticed that she was the only one naked worst than that she couldn't remember who she fucked, because the smell of sex was all over her. After that night Dawson and she began dating and she noticed how all the girls were jealous of her, because Dawson was so hot. Even though she was satisfied in dating Dawson it didn't stop her from being with Constantine, something about him made her fall in love with him she could never say no to him.

She let a week go by and still wanted to know why Kinsey did what she did, they finally sat down on Angel's bed together and Angel started to cry seconds after opening her mouth and then Kinsey started to cry.

"Angel I love you as much as my own sister and I'm sorry for what I did with Robert, I was so drunk and didn't even realize what I was doing" she said.

"Kinsey I love you too, but you know all the shit that Robert and I have gone through, its like me fucking Monroe some people are just off limits" Angel said.

She began to get very defensive and Angel noticed her face change from sorrow to anger.

"Well I wouldn't care if you slept with Monroe, because I plan on sleeping with the whole crew I already slept with nine of them, but I will leave Constantine alone if you leave Monroe alone" she said.

There were things that she confided in Angel that day that she has never before told her. Angel realized that she too hated Leon, even though she didn't tell her why, but in her heart she knew he was touching her also. The rest of the summer Kinsey and Angel had a much stronger bond than before; they seemed to spend every waking moment together. There were times that they spent the night at Constantine and Monroe's house and they would make love to them in front of each other, they had no shame, Leon stole that from them long ago.

It was the last day of summer and they still hadn't moved into the house. Angel went to the beach to see all of her friends just in case Leon decided to tell them to pack at anytime. As she laid there on the beach she noticed a shadow standing above her, it was Constantine.

"Hey baby, how much do you weigh now sweetheart it almost looks like you have a dick your pelvic bone is so far out" he said.

"Well thank you that is just what I wanted to hear from you; no I love you baby or your so sexy, it's you look like a dude!" she said.

"I'm not saying it to hurt your feelings it's just that I don't remember seeing you actually sit and eat a full meal all summer and I worry about you" he said.

Angel went home that day and for the first time in years she stood on the scale and looked at the weight. She looked down and remembered when they weighed her at school last year she weighed 103 lbs and only after three months of summer she now only weighed 78 lbs. She shrugged her shoulders and thought she probably just lost weight during the summer from walking so much, then she remembered what Constantine said about eating a meal and she also didn't remember the last time she ate a full one. It was more depressing when it was time to go school shopping and she tried on some pants and before summer she was a size one woman's and now they didn't fit her. She had to go over to the children's section and pick out some size twelve's and they fit loosely but they fit.

At school she noticed she was becoming more and more tired during classes. She started to apply foundation under her eyes to hide the bags from lack of sleep. At times her hands would start to shake uncontrollably as she wrote in her books. One day as she walked down the hall a friend of hers asked if she needed a pick me up and handed her two pills, and for the first time in a long time she refused.

"I'm trying hard to quit I'm really not feeling that great lately, thanks anyway baby" she said.

She sat in class everyday in the back and tried her hardest; she had to prove to Leon that she was smart. The days seemed like they were getting longer and the nights became shorter. She would lie in bed as Leon raped her and think of ways her life could have been better, if only she would have taken that pill an hour ago. Sometimes after he was through she would run to the bathroom and throw up. Sometimes when she ate, her body would refuse the food and throw up. This went on for a couple of months and she did try to gain weight but couldn't.

She finally made a doctors appointment at family planning, the same place where she got her birth control. She wanted to go there because they would help her without telling her parents, it was confiditional. As she laid there with only a Johnny over her she pictured herself being burned by that acid, she lifted the Johnny up and looked in the mirror on the wall beside her. She was frightened when she noticed that she could see every bone. She remembered thinking about the worst thing that Leon could do to her and that was to kill her and maybe he is winning once more. She looked as if she were already dead. She pulled the Johnny down real quick when the nurse knocked on the door.

"Angel could you please stand up on the scale so we can weigh you first, before the doctor comes to see you" the nurse said.

She blurted out "I weigh 103 pounds I weighed myself at school yesterday"

"Well we need to weigh you, every scale is different now please get up and stand here" she pointed towards the scale.

She didn't say anything as Angel stood on the scale she saw her shake her head and write 76 pounds on the paper. The doctor came in and told her to sit down they needed to talk. As she opened up her folder.

"Angel have you ever heard of bulimia? It is when a person eats food and continuously throws it up afterwards. As they do this they continue to lose more and more weight." she said.

"I don't mean to throw it up and I try to gain weight I just can't, everything I eat makes me sick" she answered.

"Do you use drugs and if so what kind, because sometimes if you use drugs your body will start to shut down from lack of healthy foods" she said.

"I have used drugs in the past, it has been about a month or two since I took any pills" Angel answered.

"You need to stay clear of the drugs, I'm going to give you some liquid medicine that will help you refrain from throwing up after your meals" she finished.

Angel went home and thought about everything the doctor had said to her about the drugs. She tried her hardest to stay off them she fought through really bad headaches, stomach aches and stress from reality. Whatever pills or weed Leon would give her she would sell to buy clothes for Summer and herself. She would not stand for Summer to be picked on because of the clothes she wore if her mom had bought them at the thrift shop.

The end of the first quarter finally arrived and she made it without drugs, she received her report card from school and saw that it helped not being on the drugs. She ran all the way home to show her mom her grades she received 2 D's and 3 C's, she was expecting her to be proud of her and all she could say was "well I hope you keep it up you don't want to stay back again do you." She took Summer out to eat that night, because she got all A's being in the first grade she knew how different it was from Kindergarten.

She started to notice her mom becoming more and more depressed again and it was all due to how bad Leon treated her and she was almost due to have Angels new baby sister or brother. Leon would still make their mom do everything for him she almost became ill when she saw her mom hold her stomach and bend over slowly to take his shoes off, or rub his feet. She would still go and clean Leonna's house and watch Kinsey and Kris all the time.

One evening as Angel and Summer were watching TV. They tried to block out the fight, Lil had just found out about another woman. Lil started yelling and calling him all sorts of names and he just stood there and his face became red, he turned around and slapped her across the face.

"See Lillian this is why I hit you, you don't know when to shut up if you learned that you wouldn't get hit so much" he yelled.

"Leon please don't I have enough problems I don't need this" she begged.

That night Lil had to go to the hospital to check on her unborn baby, while she was there Leon seemed to take his anger out on Angel. He told Summer to go into the living room and watch TV.

"Summer you sit and wait for mommy to come home so you can help her" he said.

"Angel go into the room and stay there we need to talk" he pointed to her moms bedroom, as she sat there waiting she heard him tell Summer that her sissy was in trouble and he needed to punish her.

"What did I do now, I have been trying my best" Angel said.

"You know what I want lay down and take off your clothes" he said.

"NO, Summer is right out there and I am not going to fuck you in my mom's bed while she is in the hospital because you upset her" she firmly said.

"Oh, you will do what I want you to do or we'll see what happens to Summer or your mom tonight" he said.

Angel did as he wanted then he made her get on her hands and knees while he penetrated both holes and screwed harder with every cry Angel let out. Angel put her head on the pillow and noticed the door open and Summer watching in horror.

"Sissy come here please" she cried, while holding her little hands out to her.

"I told you to stay out there didn't I, get the fuck out there and watch TV like I told you too!" he yelled.

"No I want my sissy now" she said.

"Summer I'm not saying it again get out now!" he yelled never skipping a beat on fucking Angel.

"Leon just let me bring her out and I promise I will come right back I don't want her to see me like this" Angel asked.

"No you stay right here and I will bring her out don't you move" he said.

He dragged Summer out to the living room and threw her onto the couch and she just kept yelling at him.

"Summer sissy will be alright just stay there and I will be right out sissy is alright!" Angel yelled.

"She will be alright now turning around, so I can finish "he yanked Angel around.

After that day every time that Angel would leave with Leon, Summer would cry and ask her to stay with her. Angel couldn't find the words to explain to Summer about what she saw, could only pray that she would in time forget it.

Little Brother Tony who we also called Alex

AGE 15

On January 4, 1988 Lil gave birth to Tony. Angel took Summer to the hospital with her to see their mom and baby brother. On the walk there Angel kept looking at Summer and felt so afraid that she couldn't love this new baby as much as she loved her. When they got to the hospital she took Summer aside to talk to her before going up to the room.

"Summer I want you to know that you will always be my special girl and I will never love anyone as much as you. Sometimes sissy will have to spend special time with our brother, but I will always have time for you too" Angel told her.

They walked up to the room where Lil was, and Angel held her baby brother Tony. The moment she looked into his big brown eyes she fell in love with him. He was gorgeous and looked a lot like herself. She sat and held him for about an hour and then handed him to Summer. She was so gentle with him; she kept saying "hi I'm your big sissy."

"Sissy can Tony call me Sissy like I call you?" she asked Angel.

"I'm sure he will like that, isn't he so cute?" Angel asked.

Angel left Summer at the hospital with Aunt Ann, it was way too cold to walk her back home. When she walked into the house she smelled Constantine's cologne and sure enough there he was sitting on the couch. Angel knew Leon had been gone for a couple of days so they went into her room.

"Constantine how did you get into my house?" she asked.

"Well I climbed into your bedroom window, I really needed to see you and congratulate you on your new brother" he said.

"Thanks, I wanted to talk to you also, you know that you are the only one, I have ever loved, I'm trying my best to keep straight and get my life together, and I want you to be with me" she said.

They made love that day and while they lay on her bed Angel heard the front door open. Seconds later her bedroom door opened and there stood her cousin Patrick. He came in and grabbed Constantine up by his arms. Constantine stood naked, but Patrick didn't care, he was pissed. He grabbed him and threw him up against the wall holding him by his throat.

"Do you think that you are man enough to be in the same bed as my cousin?" Patrick screamed!

"Leave him alone we love each other and it's none of your business!" Angel yelled.

"Well I'll tell you what little girl you are my family so this is my business." Patrick answered.

After that day Patrick and Angel formed a strong bond. She knew that he was the only person who cared if she got hurt or not. Her mom had never protected her from boys or men. Patrick stood by her from that day on and watched out for her. He never told Lil what he had seen that day, Constantine and Angel respected him for that. Sometimes he would just stop by to hang out or give her a ride on his bike.

At that time she was responsible for watching Summer and Tony while her mom ran errands. The winter came on quickly after Tony was born and it seemed to be colder than ever. Angel tried her best to keep Tony warm during the winter, but Leon came home and turned the heat way down saying that he was sweating. She felt so bad because sometimes his little fingers would get bright red, and she would hold them for hours it seemed. This was another way Leon controlled them, they didn't have to pay for heat it was included in the rent, they could have kept the heat on as high as they wanted.

The house still wasn't done and Angel was hoping that they might never move. She felt that if they stayed where her friends and family were, somehow, someone would see what Leon was doing to them.

Angel watched Tony take his first step and say his first words, Leon was not a real dad and their mom wasn't there to protect them, she was all Tony and Summer had. At fifteen she thought of herself as not just their sissy, but as their mom and dad as well. It was hard though, she saw Summer wrap her arms around Tony and hold him in fear of Leon in the same way she had once held her. Angel realized things would never change, her mom would never leave and she would never get out. Now there was another baby brought into their hell, and her mom had carried him into it with open arms.

Once winter came to an end and the warm weather had finally arrived, Leon wanted them to go with him out to a farm that he was taking care of while his friend was away. Angel loved animals so she agreed to go, she knew there was no choice. There were so many animals, and Leon let them know that they would be coming out here often and he would be taking over this farm one day.

The first thing that Angel wanted to see was the rabbits and there were so many of them. One had just given birth to about five bunnies. She held them and they were so little and soft, she let Summer hold one too, but not Tony because he still held things too tight. Ever since he was born he had a grip that no one had ever felt before in an infant. Leon came in and picked up a bunny and held it to his chest. Then he looked at Angel with an evil smirk, she knew he was about to do something bad. He put a finger inside of the rabbit's vagina or butt and it began to squeak in pain. "Please stop your hurting it" she cried out.

"I'm not hurting it, this is the way you tell if it is a boy or girl, this is the only way it can be done. We don't want the male next to the babies or he will eat them" he said.

As they all stood there he continued to molest this bunny in front of them. Summer stood behind Angel putting her head in the bottom of her back trying to hold back her tears. Instead of stopping when he saw that Summer was afraid he yelled at her and told her to get out. Angel knew that he did this just to get off on their pain.

When they left that day Angel saw the terror in Summers eyes, so she walked her all the way to the pet store. Angel watched as Summer held every animal that they would let her hold. She knew that this was her way of knowing that all the animals weren't afraid of people like the ones on the farm. The next week everything was back to the way it had been before. Leon, yelling and hitting their mom; mom praying that he would die the moment he left the house; knowing this would be the only way they would ever get away from him. Angel would wait up for him hoping he would just hurry and come in and do his thing. She knew after he was done raping her she could get sleep and relax maybe. If it wasn't happening all the time she would lose sleep at night wondering when it will happen again!

One weekend Patrick stopped by to see Tony, and asked if Angel wanted to go for one last ride before the summer ended.

"Ok" she answered and told her mom she would be home later.

She always let her go with Patrick knowing she would be safe. She hopped on the back of his bike and he drove to a bikers club. They sat outside with a crowd of bikers and he introduced her to everyone as his niece. Patrick and Henry where so much older than herself, no one considered them to be her cousins, they were her uncles.

"Angel ready to go, do you know of any parties so I can meet some of your friends" he asked.

"No way, you will embarrass me" she replied.

"No, I promise I just want to hang out with you for awhile" he said.

"OK, I know that my friend Alvin is having an end of the summer party, we can go over there" she said.

Once they arrived at Alvin's, she noticed that Constantine was there and he didn't say hello to her because of Patrick. Patrick walked in and puffed up his chest, like all the other guys that she had introduced him to also did. He smoked a bit of weed and then announced that if he's not around everyone should remember Angel was his niece and anyone who fucks with her, he will make sure that there life is hell.

They went home and Patrick asked Lil to sew his jeans for him. He pulled out these pants that had four of five different patches on them. He told Angel that he has had these pants since he was sixteen. They were the ugliest things she had ever seen. She gave him a hug and kissed his cheek and thanked him for the ride.

"Angel, goodbye and I love you too" he said.

That was the last time she ever saw her Uncle Patrick. Three days later he shot himself; he died beside Claudia and Cynthia's graves.

Again Angel couldn't bring herself to go to the wake or the funeral for so many reasons. The family and friends all had a party at his house and so many family members fought about this. But Henry couldn't have been more right when he said that Patrick loved to party and why not party for him one last time. After Patrick's death the family BBQ's stopped many years, no one could watch the other having fun without seeing Patrick's smile.

Angel's Aunt Talma who no one liked and never associated with Patrick, got custody of Little Patrick. No one can explain why this happened but the family never saw Little Patrick again until he turned seventeen and came home.

The end of that summer we moved into the house, walking into the living room with her mom made Angel feel guilty. She knew what happened between Leon and herself just weeks before on that very floor.

The only thing that Angel loved about the house was being able to tell people that she lived in a house and not an apartment. After showing the house to everyone, Leon brought them out back and let them know that they would have a lot of animals in the barn. Angel got quizzy she had to leave she just knew what he might be planning with the animals when they weren't there. She took a walk around the neighborhood and across the bridge to the store.

While she was over there she met a couple of guys and she knew that she would like this town. They were so gorgeous and didn't look anything alike, even though they were twins. She showed them where she lived and told them that she would love for them to show her around town. The first week in the new house went great Leon left her alone. She met and made more friends.

Starting All Over

Lil knew that Angel wouldn't go to the same school as Kinsey, so Lil signed her into her old school again. Leon agreed to pay childcare, so Lil was able to keep her job as a seamstress. Tony had a very bad temper and because of this different childcare agency in town would not take him. Lil finally had to quit her job to take care of him and again had to rely on Leon's money. She began to work odd jobs as a cleaning lady so that they could have food in the house; she worked day and night and brought Tony with her where ever she went. She tried her hardest to save money so that she could leave him. Angel would listen to her mom complain in the middle of the night while she cleaned her own house because this was the only time she had left to do her house work.

Meredith went to Angel one day and told her that a discount store opened up next to Mc Donald's and they were looking for help.

"Angel it will be so cool we could have money again and help our moms out" she said.

"We have to be at least sixteen to have a job, not fifteen" Angel replied.

"We will dress up, well down if you know what I mean and say that we are sixteen" she said grabbing her boobs.

Angel knew what she meant when she dress down, that meant dress sluttish and if it is a man they would get the job. That weekend Angel had Lil drop them off at the store and were dressed in both high heels and skirts. Walking into the store Angel became a little nervous but as soon as she saw that this guy was in his early thirties with a manager's badge on his shirt she was sure they would get hired.

"Hello sir, my friend and I are looking for a job working nights and weekends" Angel said extending her hand out.

"Are you both over the age of sixteen?" he asked.

"Well yes I wouldn't be here if I wasn't" Angel replied.

"We are very hard workers and follow instructions well" Meredith said.

The whole time they sat there he kept looking them up and down.

"OK girls fill out this paper work to the best of your knowledge and you are hired" he said.

"Thank you so much" Angel said smiling.

Going to school was Angel's way to escape from the hell that she endured at home. At the beginning of the school year Leon had brought home some animals; they had geese, baby bulls, horses, sheep and a huge pig. Most of the time Angel would get up around five and go feed them. Her favorites were the bulls, she had a hard time feeding them though, so Leon invented this bucket like thing that attached to her waist and it had a nipple on it. Angel would wrap it around her and the bulls would start to suck on the nipple and pull her around the yard. Sometimes she would have to wiggle out of the belt and run away but it was fun. At times Lil would get up with her and try to feed the pig and Angel would laugh so hard when it would get out and they had to chase it around.

Physically and mentally Angel was as stable as she could have been with what she had to endure. She gained a little weight and was off the drugs for awhile. She wanted to prove to her mom that she could do well in school again like when they moved to Milton. She did work very hard and only dated guys, but she wouldn't do anything with them, only hung out. It was like moving to Northfield changed her and gave her a better reputation and more self esteem. Her first report card of the semester showed that her hard work paid off with B's and C's.

It wasn't long before Leon began to be himself again. He became very distant from Lil and every that she needed to talk to someone; she would find her car not running and was stuck away from family and friends. The more fights they had the more Angel started to miss school and the harder she would have to work to catch up on the homework. She lost the job that she had, because the guy was reported to the state for hiring minors. She knew that she needed a job though, because she had to save money for a car. Angel started at Shaws as a bagger and then after only one month she began to cashier. Angel loved going to work; if the car didn't work she had the money to take a cab.

There was a day when Angel didn't have cab money and she needed a ride to work, she asked Lil to give her a ride, Lil told her that she was to sick to drive her and would have to bring her. Angel walked to the barn to look for him and saw the barn door shut but heard his voice. She opened the door slowly and saw Leon standing there with his pants around his ankles. In front of him was one of the sheep and she was tied up to the post. He turned around and for what Angel thought would have been an embarrassing moment for him it seemed as though he could care less.

"You know Angel, sheep's pussy is almost identical to a woman's pussy but tighter" he said.

He finished and pulled his pants up acting as though nothing happened. He brought Angel to work and all the way there she wanted to ask him again why he would do that to an innocent animal. Every time she would open her mouth nothing came out. He didn't say anything, Angel was sure he didn't expect anyone to walk in on him. While at work all she could do was picture that poor sheep tied up and being raped the same way she had been for years. Angel knew just then that she was no better than the animals that Leon owned. After work she went to the barn and checked up on the sheep it wasn't there and she looked all around for it.

"Leon do you know where the sheep went" she asked.

"It was its time I had to put it down for food" he answered.

Angel knew why he killed it; it was because if she told anyone then there may be evidence on the sheep that they could find. She also knew that from now on she would have to volunteer to feed the animals so that he couldn't get to them and hurt them.

Other than Leon, things seemed to be going ok. She started to learn how to drive from Lil and she let her drive everywhere they went. Grades became less and less important because her focus was getting her license and driving away with Summer and Alex somewhere that Leon couldn't find them. As her grades started to slip she had more pressure from Lil and the school and her way out again became drugs.

There were times that she would spend the day taking Lils car while she was at work and checking out towns that she knew she could hide in. School would call her mom and ask her where she was, when she asked Angel she always was quick to have an answer, either she was helping Leon or she was home sick and she just didn't see her.

Her sixteenth birthday was coming up and there was a new club opening up in Belmont and she started to spend her weekends there and met a lot of new friends. With new friends came new drugs and parties. Outside of home she focused on nothing but where she would get more drugs at and forget about home, then when she was home all she concentrated on was trying to get out. But in order to get out of hell she would have to become numb to all the pain Leon put her through.

It was a nice day out and Leon wanted Angel to learn how to handle a truck in hopes that when she got her license she would be working for him and driving the trucks back and forth with logs to customers.

"Angel how do you expect to get a car" he asked.

"Well I've been saving some money up from work" she answered.

"I have to get Kinsey and you a car in a few months but which one of you will deserve the better car" he said.

They went to a car dealership and looked at cars, Angel found an awesome 1988 Ferrari it was red and sporty, just her type she thought.

"Go and get my briefcase behind the seat of the truck" Leon said.

"Here what's in it" Angel asked as she passed it to him.

"Stay here I have something for you" he said.

She sat and watched as he seemed to smooth talk the dealer and then handed him a wad of cash. As the dealer counted three stacks of cash, Leon sat and gave his famous grin towards Angel, just then she thought for sure she had the car.

"Angel did you see what I just did" he asked.

"You bought me a car, so what do I need to do before I get it" she asked.

"Lets take a drive around and we will discuss it" he said.

As they drove around he explained how Kinsey did everything that she won't do for him.

"Well I'm not Kinsey and I believe that I have done plenty for you over the years and deserve a hell of a lot more than a car" she said.

"You have a choice here, with a little loving you can have a $6,000.00 car or be a little bitch and get a $500.00 car" he said.

She went to school that next week and the school year was almost over and she couldn't remember going more than half the year. Lil was sitting in the principal's office one day and they both wanted to talk to Angel.

"Do you know why your mom is here?" The principal asked.

"No" she answered.

"Well I've been looking at your work and with your grades your going to stay back again or you can choose to quit and get your GED someday when your willing to do the work" he said.

It was just that easy and Angel quit school at fifteen and a half. She was hoping that Lil would maybe step in and say no but she didn't hesitate to sign the papers. It seemed now Leon had more reasons to work her and Lil had a built in babysitter.

Angel's sixteenth birthday was coming up in a couple of months and her Dad called her and said that he would definitely be there for this birthday. Meanwhile, Leon gave Angel clothes to wear and told her she would have to paint the storage shed the clothes were a bikini top and daisy duke shorts. Angel would see him from the corner of her eye jerking off in his truck while he sat there and watched her. She wanted that car so bad just so she could leave him behind if bending alittle more for him helped then it didn't compare to what he had already done to her.

At work she met this guy that came through her line with a friend one day, minutes later his friend Jon who Angel knew for a couple of years came back and told her that his friend Dwayne would like her to go to a party at his house. When she drove to the address after work Dwayne was sitting on the couch and asked her to sit and talk with him. She did and he said he had been watching her for a while and thought that she was beautiful and looked so pure. Angel thought to herself that what he was saying was a joke she hasn't been pure since she was six. They had a few drinks and smoked some weed then they went upstairs.

Dwayne undressed her so gently and kissed her all over. They had sex and the whole time his friend Jon was banging on the door. For the first time in a long time she felt safe with someone. She overheard Dwayne tell his friends downstairs that from the moment he saw her years ago he knew they would end up together. Angel tried her best to remember him but couldn't. She was still at the time dating Dawson and believed that she still loved him and she explained this to Dwayne and he wrapped his arms around her and told her that he would wait for her.

Meredith and Angel went to the club that weekend and Dwayne and Dawson were there, Dawson had asked Angel to dance with him and the song "Patience" from Guns and Roses was playing and she thought it was just right for the moment.

"Dawson I have met someone else and you have a pregnant girlfriend anyway and I think you should try to work that out" she said.

"You know that I love you baby, but listen to this song and know that I will wait for you, we will be together again someday" he said.

They kissed and that was the end of Dawson and Angel, Angel went and danced with Dwayne after Dawson had left. Dwayne was described as a quiet person with long curly hair, tight jeans and ripped at the knees and always wore cowboy boots. Angel loved how sensitive he was and how he looked like a "bad boy". That same night he drove her home and met Lil, she said she really liked him he seemed very polite. Dwayne and Angel talked every day and became really close.

Her Sweet Sixteen

AGE 16

Her birthday had finally arrived and she awoke hoping to see a car waiting for her outside and that night there would be a huge sweet sixteen birthday party or so she thought. Weeks went by and still there wasn't a car and her mom finally remembered her birthday, and her dad finally called. Angel finally got a Happy Birthday hug from her mom and she wasn't expecting anything else because they had no money, but she could have remembered to say it anyway. Her Dad didn't come by until June because he told her that Katrina had been sick and he needed to plan a day to come down.

It was boiling hot one day at the end of August and Angel had to go to work, but her mom was too sick to bring her and told her to go and find Leon to drive her. He was in the barn and as she opened the door he was startled. Angel asked him why all the animals were outside it was too hot for them.

"Angel today I am going to help you celebrate a late birthday, I know that you didn't get much of a birthday" Leon said.

"No that's all right Leon I just need to go to work" Angel replied.

"No you don't I called them and told them that there was a family emergency so we could celebrate, come in here and shut the door we need to talk" he said.

Angel walked in and Leon locked the door. He walked towards the back and picked up a couple of pieces of rope. Angel became very nervous looking at the rope; she noticed it was the same kind that he had tied the sheep up with.

"Angel turn around and take off your cloths, I have a surprise for you" he said smiling.

"Please Leon I really just want to go to work" she said.

"Do what I say and I will try to be gentle" he commanded.

Angel stripped down and turned around as he held up the rope.

"Get up against the gate and bend over it, put your head in between the top and second slabs of wood " he told her.

Angel did as he said and he pulled her hands down to meet her ankles on the other side of the gate and tried to tie them together. She tried to move and he slapped her ass telling her that he wasn't joking around. He spread her legs and tied her ankles and wrist to the bottom of the gate. She cried silently when she realized she was in the same position as the sheep when he raped her.

"Angel remember when I told you that a sheep's pussy was much like a woman's and you didn't believe me. Well what do you think now? Don't answer that, I can tell looking at your pussy right now that they are the same"

She tried to hold in the vomit as she smelled the slop from the huge pig in the corner looking at her. She new if she threw up he would just put her face in it and at that moment there wasn't much separating her from the pig. He held Angels hair and raped her over and over again then finished inside her. Looking down at his penis she noticed he wasn't wearing a condom.

"Happy Birthday Angel and don't worry this isn't the only gift I'm going to give you, I'm taking you shopping tonight and you can pick out some clothes" he said untying her.

Later on her mother noticed the marks on her ankles and told her that she needed to wear different shoes, ones that won't leave marks. Leon came home at around six that night and asked her if she wanted to go shopping for her birthday. Of course she said yes to going shopping, her mom didn't care and her dad didn't send her anything. They drove all the way to the Fox Run Mall and she picked out an awesome white leather skirt and jacket. It cost $150.00 and Leon agreed to buy it for her.

"Also pick out a bathing suit, summer is here and I haven't seen a new bathing suit in awhile and you have grown so much since last year" he said.

She picked out a cute red and white bikini and felt good about finally being able to shop outside the kids section. On the way home they made a stop and she wasn't surprised to see that they were at a hotel, there had to be someway she paid Leon back for the clothes.

"I think that it is about time for you to show me some appreciation for all that I have done for you" he said.

"I thought you got this for my birthday and I didn't think that I would have to pay you back or I wouldn't have gotten so much" Angel said hesitantly.

"I did get it for your birthday but I deserve something for bringing you all the way here, stay in the truck till I get back" then with the slam of the door he was gone.

Angel sat up and looked at the hotel; it was something that you would have seen in a horror movie, slime green shutters, dingy white exterior with the paint looking as though it was melting off the building. She looked at the window and inside saw an old man sitting at his desk and by the looks of him Leon had just awoken him. As the man looked back at Angel she ducked and realized that she was playing into Leon's games, he had her hiding from society.

He came back and they walked into the room and he sat on the bed then told her to get her bathing suit on and show him how it fits. She started towards the bathroom when he stopped her and told her to strip there. As she stood there she pictured how it would feel if she were to be strong and tell him no.

"No I won't let you rape me not here and not anywhere else" she said as she stood naked with her back facing him.

She felt him brush against her and she tried to walk away, he grabbed her and threw her to the ground her breast hitting the floor. She pushed her arms up, and then he slammed her down pushing all the air out of her.

"Don't you ever tell me no you little bitch" he said wrapping his hands around her neck.

She fought it for a minute then felt her body give into him and she prayed that he would kill her, and she would finally be free. She felt the blood rush to her head then he released his grip slowly and the blood began to flow back into her again. She wasn't happy that she still was alive, to feel the pain that he was going to give to her. She was mad that she didn't stand her ground, she had failed again. They stood up and he pushed her onto the bed and raped her, she closed her eyes and again tried to picture someone else. Again he hadn't wore a condom and he had finished inside her this made her so sick she turned her head and threw up. Leon found this as the biggest insult to his sex making so he slapped Angel over and over again, she held her hands out while trying not to choke on her vomit. He picked her up and threw her into the bathtub bending her over, holding her head under the faucet.

"Please let me take a shower I can do it myself, gurgling on the water" she cried.

"No you little bitch you wasted enough of my time" he yelled yanking her out of the tub her hair dripping wet.

They finally made it home and she smiled as she turned her head towards him "Leon I hope that you enjoyed yourself because to be honest I am too old for this shit. This will be the last time that you touch me" Angel said fiercely.

As they walked towards the house she could feel her heart racing and her skin getting hot. She didn't cry, she couldn't show him how afraid she was. All the way down the driveway she pictured what he might do to her mom, Summer or Alex this time. She walked in and her mom was sitting at the table with a cake in front of her. She must of felt bad because Leon had done something for her daughter's birthday and she hadn't.

"Mom you didn't have to get me a cake all I wanted on my birthday was a simple "Happy Birthday" and a hug and kiss" she said.

"Angel I am so sorry for forgetting your birthday, just so many things have been going on lately" her mom said.

If only she had known while she was worried about what kind of cake to get her daughter, or what she should say to her, that her man was raping her daughter again. The next day when Angel walked outside there was a Ford Escort parked in front of the house with a $400.00 sign on it.

"Angel this is your birthday gift from me" Leon said.

Angel was pissed because she knew she got this car instead of the Ferrari because she was fighting with him every time he tried to touch her. That night Kinsey drove to the house in this fancy Camero that Leon had bought for her. Angel left as soon as Kinsey was finished showing off and she went to pick up Meredith and they drove back to the house. They sat on the top of the car and took pictures of themselves posing making sure Leon watched from the window, and he knew he didn't get to her again.

A week later she went to the barn and told Leon that she wanted to move out and she had been saving up money to do so. He took her arms and dragged her inside the barn and slammed her against the barn door.

"This will be the last time I fuck you then, and I will make sure you don't forget it!" he said.

He raped her so hard and again with out a condom then finished inside her. She was just relieved that he said this would be the last time.

A few weeks went by and she went down to see Dawson one last time and they smoked a joint then he asked her to make love to him and she did. She then went to Dwayne's house that next week and told him that she wanted to stay with him and she was finally done with everyone else. That month she was so happy because she knew that she planned on being with only Dwayne and it was the first relationship that she had that wasn't involving Leon at all.

For the next month or so she stayed clear of Leon and her mom, she didn't know how to tell her mom that she wanted to move out. One night before she went to bed she had taken off her cloths to put on her pajamas and noticed that they fit a little snug, she ran downstairs and her mom rubbed her belly and mentioned that she was getting a little pudgy. She ran upstairs and undressed and rubbed her stomach as she looked in the full length mirror on the inside of the door. Her mom was right but what she didn't say is that all the fat was in her stomach area. As the months went by she still was gaining weight and hardly eating anything. She thought that maybe it's just that she had been drinking more and more alcohol and she now had a car and wasn't walking as much. The question did come to mind that she might be pregnant but she still was getting her period every month she hadn't skipped any. She finally broke down and bought a pregnancy test, she went into the stores bathroom. She screamed as she looked down and the test showed that she was indeed pregnant. So many questions came to Angels mind, could it be Dawson's or Dwayne's, no they wore a condom every time, but people say that a condom can break it could be his. While she sat on the toilet in a dingy bathroom at a local store she cried out "Oh my god I'm pregnant with that bastard's child."

Her Baby

Just like some other teenagers that get pregnant the biggest fear Angel had was telling her parents. She made an appointment at Family Planning in hope that the test from the store might be wrong. Her appointment to find out her future was the next day. She drove her car to the office and parked she walked upstairs feeling as though she could faint at anytime. Her hands shook as she opened the door and handed the cup to the nurse who had given it to her the day before.

"Is this for a pregnancy test or something else?" she asked.

Angel stood still for a moment then finally answered as her lips began to tremble.

"Yes I'm here for a pregnancy test. My name is Angel and I may be pregnant" she said.

She realized that she sounded like one of those commercials for teen parents. She sat in a room feeling more alone than she had ever felt before. She followed the same nurse who had helped her before with the warts into the room. The nurse sat across from her and began to shake her head back and forth.

"Angel dear I hate to be the bearer of this kind of news. You are pregnant and we can find out how far along you are" she said.

She sat there in shock not knowing what to do or say, she couldn't move for what seemed like hours.

"Did you hear what I said sweetie?" the nurse repeated.

"Yes, how can that be, I still have my period I never missed any, what am I going to do" she asked knowing that there was nothing she could do to change her circumstances.

"Well, the first thing you need to do is tell your parents then there are options we can help you with. Some women will spot throughout their whole pregnancy, its more common then people might think" she said.

"Well, if you mean abortion or adoption, that is not an option for me, I will keep this baby, I just don't know how to deal with it" Angel answered her.

"OK dear get undressed and I will examine you then we will be able to determine from your last full period how far along you are" she said as she handed her a Johnny and walked out the door.

Angel got undressed and looked at her naked body in the mirror this thing in her stomach looked bigger than ever. The examination was over and the questions were answered, she was thirteen weeks pregnant. She didn't understand how she couldn't know she was pregnant for three months. The nurse handed her a letter that was addressed to her mom. It was letting her know that she was if fact pregnant and would need follow up visits with her OBGYN.

She left the office and in her heart and mind she knew that being thirteen weeks pregnant the baby belonged to that monster "Leon". He must have gotten her pregnant that time in the hotel room or the barn. She thought what a birthday gift he had given her for her sixteenth birthday.

She went to the high school and waited for Meredith to get out of school, nearly four hours went by before Meredith was finally sitting in her car.

"What's wrong Angel, I can tell something is up you've been crying?" she asked.

"Meredith I am pregnant what am I going to do?" Angel asked hoping that Meredith might have all the answers.

"Whose baby is it, is it Dawson's or Dwayne's" she asked.

"Well the baby couldn't belong to Dawson I am thirteen weeks along. Dwayne wore a condom, but there is a small chance that the baby belongs to him" she answered. She couldn't tell Meredith who the baby might have belong to.

"Do you want me to be there when you tell your mom, you are going to tell your mom aren't you, I will be there for you I'm your best friend" she said.

"No I have to tell her myself, but will you be there when I go to talk with Dwayne, I want to talk to him first then mom" she asked.

On the drive to Dwayne's house, all she could do was cry. They had become so close over the last couple of months and she didn't want to loose him. She snuck by his mom who was in the kitchen at the time, and

Meredith held her hand as they walked upstairs to his bedroom. Dwayne still lived with his mom Cheryl and his dad Roger. He also had three brothers but only one of them lived with him and his name was Lance.

"Dwayne are you in there" she asked knocking on the door her heart pounding inside her chest.

"Yeah come in Baby" he answered.

She walked in and sat on the bed and he held her knee while it continued to shake.

"What's wrong, why are you crying" he asked.

"Dwayne I'm not sure how to tell you this, I'm pregnant and I'm going to keep the baby and you have a choice to make. You can leave me and I won't be mad, just hurt, or you can stay and be this baby's daddy. There is something else you have to know if the doctors are right about the time, you are not the father" she explained.

He pulled her closer to him and hugged her so tight and told her that he would be with her forever.

"Stay right here I'll be right back" he said and then he left. He was gone for a little while.

"Angel come with me we will go for a ride, Meredith you can come with us" he said.

She didn't hesitate they went to his car to go for a ride. His car was this beaten up crayon yellow station wagon and on the inside everyone who rode with him signed their names on the roof or on the doors.

"Angel can you please get me a smoke their in the side of the door" he asked.

She looked for them and noticed "Angel I love you" written in black magic marker on the door handle. Then, Dwayne put his hand on hers and squeezed it.

"Oh I love you too Dwayne" she said.

Later that night she asked her mom if they could go out to eat or for ice cream. She figured if she told her mom the news in public she couldn't yell at her or cause a scene.

"Angel I'm happy that we are alone I needed to talk to you about something. We are going to move far away from him, I can't take it anymore" she said as her eyes began to tear up.

"No, mom I can't move with you I need to stay here" Angel pleaded as the young teenage blonde waitress came to take their order.

"You are only sixteen so you have to move with me" she said.

"Mom, you know how the other day you said that I was getting a bit chunky, well it's because I am pregnant" she answered as the waitress stood for a moment and then just walked away after neither one of them placed an order.

"You're lying your not pregnant" she said with a stern tone.

"Yes I am, I have a letter to prove it from Family Planning" Angel said.

"Let's go we have to go to Kmart to get a few things" she said ignoring all Angel had just said.

They drove to the store without talking, and it was completely silent as they walked into the store. Lil picked up a rattle and handed it to Angel.

"Well, what's done is done. I will tell you though if you are going to keep the baby you will raise it yourself! If you need me to raise the baby I will, but the baby will be mine not yours" she said giving Angel a hug.

Angel went and saw Dwayne a couple of days after telling her mom and they agreed that she needed to get away from Leon. They talked to his mom and she agreed that Angel could move in. The next step was to have a plan if she moved out who would protect Summer and Alex. Then, she would have to tell her mom again and that she needed to move out.

"Angel do you want me to be there when you tell your mom" Dwayne asked.

"No, I need to tell her alone, I will call you later" she said as she kissed him, hoping everything would be alright.

She walked into the house and saw that everyone was there; Alex ran up to her and hugged her legs. She looked at his huge puppy dog brown eyes and broke down and cried.

"Angel what's wrong, Sweetie" Lil asked.

"Can I talk to you alone please" she asked her mom while looking at Leon hoping he wouldn't make her talk in front of him.

They walked upstairs to Angel's room and sat on the end of the bed.

"Mom I love you, but I want to move out, no I have to move out, I will be back to get all of you away from him. I need to save myself first before I can help you" she said and they both started to cry.

"It's ok you move out as long as you are sure Dwayne will treat you right" she said tearfully.

Angel went downstairs knowing she had to break the news to Summer and Alex, but Leon was yelling about something as usual.

"Lillian in here now" he yelled.

Angel went into the kitchen where he was and noticed Alex had made a mess, there was food everywhere. Leon bent down and screamed into

Alex's face making him scoot himself into a corner, he looked just like China did when Leon would yell at him. Summer went to Alex and held his ears the same way Angel used to hold hers and told Leon to shut up. Alex began to scream and cry as his body began to shake out of control.

"Get that kid in the other room and clean up this mess" he yelled pointing towards Lil and then the floor.

"Summer please take brother into the other room, sissy will be in there in a couple of minutes. Angel said walking them into the living room.

"Leon please calm down its just a little food I will clean it up" Lil pleaded.

He turned and back handed her across the face causing her to fall against the wall then to the floor. Angel didn't know what came over her next, maybe it was the raging hormones she heard other pregnant woman talk about, or seeing her mom fall to the floor again from him hitting her, but she yelled at the top of her lungs.

"Shut the hell up and go and take a nap you fuckin' pig" pointing towards him and then the stairs."

She looked at her moms' face, the fear in her eyes not knowing what he may do to her daughter for yelling at him. He swung around and with the back of his hand he slapped Angel across the neck and she flew into the stove then fell to the floor as she saw her mom do so many times. Angel blacked out because the next thing she remembered was standing next to the sink, she picked up a glass and threw it at him hoping that it hit him hard enough to kill him. She missed and it hit the wall next to his head, but it was enough to make him walk away.

For the first time ever she saw he was puzzled, he looked as though he didn't know what to do. As he walked out she knew they all were thinking the same thing that this would be the end; he would be gone forever. He did stay away for two days, while he was gone Angel begin to pack her things.

Dwayne didn't waste any time coming to pick her up after she called him and told him that she was all packed. She gave her last kisses to everyone in that house. She promised Summer and Alex that she would be back for them real soon. Lil acted as though it would be her last time seeing Angel. And in Angels mind there was a chance it may have been the last time she saw them alive, she wouldn't be there for him to take the abuse out on anymore. As she walked out Leon was just pulling in and Angel stood there and thought to herself that this must be a sick joke that God was playing on her. Knowing that this was her escape and here he comes towards the car. She was also thinking that it was God that put Dwayne there on that very day.

"Angel where do you think you're going" he said.

"She's moving in with me and she won't be back" Dwayne said loud and clear.

"I will be back to get mom, sis and my little brother away from you and see that you get everything that you deserve you sick bastard" Angel said.

"Oh really" he replied.

"One more thing if you lay another hand on any of them I will see that the next time I see you it will be at your funeral. I will be the one throwing the dirt over you. I promise you that, and unlike you I never break my promises" she said.

They drove off and went back to Dwayne's house to unpack Angel's things. Lying in her new bed and on Dwayne's arm that night she felt safer than she had ever felt before yet she couldn't sleep. She lay in his arms feeling guilty for leaving the rest of them with that monster. She wasn't there to protect them; she knew that she had to work as quickly as possible to save them.

She knew what she had to do that next morning. She had to go to the police and tell them everything. She questioned if they would believe her, would she be talking to a cop that he knew and maybe paid off like he said he did. These questions kept her up all night. She first had to talk to her mom and wait to make sure she was safe knowing that if she told he may get away with it and they would be in danger more than ever.

Angel also knew that she had to tell Dwayne everything that Leon had done to her family, that way he wouldn't find out some other way. It was so hard for Angel to tell him; although there were things she kept to herself things that humiliated even her. After she was done she expected a disgusted look across his face, but he amazed her even more when he hugged her and cried with her for hours. She could see only compassion in his eyes for what she had gone through. He reassured her that what ever she had to do to save everyone from Leon he would be there for her.

The Statement And Marriage

A week went by before Angel called her mom and she reassured her that Leon hadn't touched any of them since she had left. Angel knew that she would have to work as fast as possible to make sure he never touched any of them again.

The next day she went to the police station, her chest sinking, and it hurt to breathe, walk or even move. She looked around and wondered which officer's life she wanted to change with her story. Most of all, which officers did Leon, own she thought. She saw this friendly face coming towards her, he looked like Ponch from the TV show CHIPS, and the officers' name was Officer Moyer. Angel asked him if he would sit to talk with her while she told him the things that her step father had done to her.

They walked into a small room with cream colored walls, black leather seats, a typing machine and recorder. Angel sat in the chair that looked most comfortable and Officer Moyer sat across from her.

"Would it be ok if I had a lady come in and type the things that you want to tell me, this way we could help you much better" he asked.

"Sure" Angel answered.

She felt an instant sweat begin on her neck and forehead as she began to speak.

"My name is Angel and my step fathers name is Leon, and he touches me" she blurted out.

Angel only looked up once as she continued with her story and that was enough to see the disgust on Officer Moyer's face. She wasn't sure why but she felt ashamed, embarrassed and guilty for what she had let Leon do to her. She knew in the back of her mind that she wasn't to blame for the horrific things he had done to her, but the look on the faces around her made her believe different.

Angel tried to tell everything but some things were just too embarrassing. Officer Moyer reassured her that Leon would be arrested as long as she signed the papers. Not ever meeting this Officer before he had that look in his eyes that gave a silent promise that everything would be ok. Now all that was left was to wait and hear from the police they said they would call her.

That night her mom called and frantically told her how the police came and arrested Leon. Angel knew that this was only the beginning before it would be over. No sooner had she started to feel some peace in her heart when the very next morning her mom called to tell her that Leon was out on bail. He was ordered to stay out of the house until the case went to court, he moved in with his dad at the garage. Angel didn't know how to feel, she was relieved everyday to hear that he didn't stop by the house, yet something in her heart was telling her that he was planning something horrible.

The police called Angel and told her that she would have to go to the court house and talk to a lady whose name was Barbara. Little did she know that this would be the woman who would change the rest of her life? The first thing Angel noticed was how frail this woman looked standing in front of her with her mousy, brown hair, thick glasses and pale skin Angel wondered how in the world was this weak looking woman going to help her fight Leon in court. As soon as Barbara began to talk her words mesmerized Angel and the tone of her voice was strong and reassuring.

"Angel I am here for you I have read the statement you gave to the police and I want you to know that none of this was your fault and we will make sure that he gets what he deserves" she said.

Seeing the fight in her eyes Angel knew that she meant it and she believed her.

"Now tell me everything start from the first time he touched you" she asked.

Angel started talking just as she had with Officer Moyer but it was easier to tell Barbara her story. Barbara sat across from her and held her hands and Angel shook with every word. Hours went by and she listened and didn't judge Angel; just listened.

"I just need to save mom, Summer and Alex" Angel told her.

"I will help you when the trial begins and I will be with you the whole time, but I have to tell you that it may take weeks, months or even years before he goes to jail, there are a lot of things we have to do first and it will get harder before it gets easier" she said.

Angel knew that there was one thing very important that she had left out and that was she was pregnant, and the baby she was carrying most likely belonged to Leon. As months went by Angel began to show more and more. She tried to hide it but her body started to confirm that she indeed may be pregnant with that monsters child.

Every time she went down to the court another layer of clothing would hide her belly, amazing enough no one in the court questioned her about being pregnant.

One night Angel sat in the window of Dwayne's bedroom, she was fascinated by how beautiful the world looked on the outside.

"Please Lord I know that I don't call upon you like most people do and how you must have been to busy to keep that demon off from me. But I am begging you Lord, please, if this is his baby take it from me now, I don't think I could ever love something that belonged to him the way you would want me to, please Lord this time answer my prayer" she begged.

She felt nothing, she wanted to end this herself because again she believed the Lord had left her, she picked up a hand full of pills and took them hoping that the pills would end the baby's life. She laid on the bed and started to fade just as Dwayne's face appeared above her and she watched as he rubbed her belly and kissed it and he whispered to the baby "No matter who put you in your moms tummy you will always belong to me I will be your Daddy and she will love you regardless of who put you there in the first place".

She then faded into a deep sleep and when she woke up the next morning with Dwayne beside her, she didn't feel any morning sickness. Could the Lord have granted her prayer, did he take her baby away from this awful hell that she might bring it into, did he bring the baby to a life of happiness and away from all the pain that it may have to go through with Leon. Angel couldn't move her body, it was numb and she laid in bed for hours, telling Dwayne that she was just sick and needed to rest. She remembered the doctors telling her that if she started bleeding, she may be having a miscarriage. There was no sign of blood and she didn't know if she was still pregnant or not. She began to beg during those hours and asked the Lord if he wanted her to keep the baby then show her a sign.

While she laid there her body suddenly became so weak that she couldn't move her arms or legs and then she started to feel her inside. The baby began to move and kick, it was the first time she had felt the baby. She knew that this was a sign from the Lord telling her that the baby should live. She finally began to feel the rest of her body. She made a promise to the Lord that she would never take any pills that weren't prescribed to her again and she would never try to take her own life. She would do everything in her power to make sure that her baby comes out healthy. The Lord gave her baby the chance to live and she would have to do the same.

All that night the baby kicked and Dwayne was able to feel it also. The Lord gave this baby to her to save her life and it was as if this baby was her Angel, someone there to let her know that life is worth living no matter what you have to go through to live it.

Things started to unwind; she began having many appointments with different Lawyers and told each one of them her story. A week after the last deposition a court date was set, it was scheduled for one month later.

She went to work and as she was bagging some groceries she thought of Leon and court and began to feel faint. The next thing she knew she was laying in someone's arms being carried to the manager's office. She called Dwayne and he was there right away and he drove her to the hospital.

"Angel your babies heart is racing this is telling us that your baby is under a lot of stress. You will need to take a leave from work, not complete bed rest but no straining" the doctor advised.

The following day she went to work and let them know that she needed the rest of her pregnancy off, and her boss surprisingly, was fine with that. As she walked out into the hallway she noticed Dwayne smiling and he asked her to sit for a minute they needed to talk. He got on one knee and she knew what he would say next. She began to cry.

"Angel I fell in love with you from the moment our eyes met and I want us to be together for the rest of our lives. Will you do me the honor and be my wife?" he asked.

"Of course" she responded.

When they got home she asked him "why in the hall way of Shaw's".

"I would have asked you anywhere but I wanted that bitch Marie to see it" he answered. Marie was his first fiancée, he was with her for three years and she left him, now she was Angel's boss.

They both took their time telling Angels mom and his parents about the engagement. When they finally did they all seemed very happy. Lil told Angel that she would have to call her Dad and tell him herself. With all that was going on she realized she hadn't even told her Dad that she was pregnant yet.

Angel made the call and told him about the baby and engagement. He started to cry so she didn't think it would be the right time to tell him about Leon too. In her heart she still blamed him also for what Leon did. If he never cheated on her Mom then she wouldn't have moved away and ended up with Leon. Also, she thought how could a Dad see his daughter time and time again and not know that she was being abused.

She began to panic because things were moving too fast with the marriage but she wanted to be married before the baby was born. They set a date for February 24, 1990.

They made arrangements that her dad would walk her down the aisle. Meredith would be her maid of honor and Tara would be one of the many brides' maids.

Lil was eager to help any way she could. They went to many stores looking at wedding gowns that were out of Angel's price range. They finally stopped at the Etcetera shop, it was like the Salvation Army, or second hand stores.

"Oh my God mom, look at this wedding gown its perfect" Angel yelled.

"It is beautiful but by the time the wedding is here you will be 7 months pregnant and this gown is too small already" she said.

Angel knew she was right but she didn't want to admit that she was too fat to fit into it. When they got home she called Aunt Phyllis because she wanted Vallerie to be in the wedding. Aunt Phyllis said yes; she would make sure that Vallerie was there, as long as William could be an usher. After all that happened between William and Angel, she couldn't see having him as an usher or even at her wedding. Vallerie had her old prom dress and she would sell it to Angel for two hundred dollars. Angel couldn't pass it up; Lil said that she would pay for it being she may only be able to help Angel with that financially. The gown did look like a wedding dress, it would have to be altered to fit Angel's pregnant belly though.

They went back to the Etcetera shop two weeks later and found matching dresses for the maids of honor and bride maids as well. Everything was going as planned, they now needed to see the pastor of the church and get his permission to have the wedding there. Angel was Protestant and Dwayne was Catholic, she was only sixteen and pregnant, Angel could only imagine what he would say. He agreed to marry them in the church as long as they went to weekly meetings with him, something like counseling. He was certain after talking with them a few times that they would be happy and they were doing the right thing for the baby.

Later that week they had another ultrasound and the nurse told them that they were in fact having a baby boy. Dwayne told everyone he was going to have a baby boy, he was so proud because, after all, most men want a baby boy. This news helped Angel relax a bit because Leon wouldn't molest a boy, so her baby would be safe if Leon was still around.

She thought everything was set for the wedding. She began to get all of these calls from people telling her that they wouldn't be able to make the wedding for some lame reason or another. She let Aunt Phyllis know that things worked out and William could be in the wedding after all. Angel figured if the Lord forgave her for her sins and was giving her a chance to get married in his house that she could forgive someone also. Leonna called and said if she was going to make all the bouquets that instead of payment, Angel should let Kinsey and Kris in the wedding. Also her dad called and said if Summer and Alex were going to be in the wedding then she should have Colby and Katrina too. Angel knew that she no longer was planning her wedding everyone else was doing it for her.

Finally the rehearsal day was there, Angel had planned it the day before the wedding so that way everyone could be there instead of traveling twice in the snow. Everyone showed up except Meredith and Tara. They all started to pace up and down becoming irritated because, after all, they had to wait for the Maid of Honor. After two hours of waiting the rehearsal finally started without them. The following day Angel got a hold of Meredith and was appalled to hear what Meredith had to say

"Meredith what's going on" Angel asked hoping she was very ill because any other reason wouldn't have been acceptable.

"Angel, Tara and I talked it over and we can't be there today, we can't see you marry Dwayne knowing that you aren't really happy. We don't like him and he doesn't treat you the way you should be treated. We love you and hope that your wedding is great and that you will be happy" she said hanging up the phone.

Angel had to talk to Dwayne about what just happened, but she couldn't tell him why. He calmed her down and told her that she needed to find someone to fit into Merediths and Taras dresses, that way the wedding party would be even men to women. She called around and Lori Lance's girlfriend who Angel couldn't stand said Dwayne had already asked her and she agreed to be in the wedding, then she could be with Lance. Angel asked Kinsey to be her maid of honor and she could fit into the dress, so that wasn't to bad. Then she needed to find someone to fit into Kinsey's dress there was only Christine which was one of Denise's nieces.

Angel started to walk up the stairs of the church and couldn't help noticing that the wedding wasn't hers, it belonged to everyone else. The church was beautiful though and Dwayne was so handsome in his grey tux. As she walked down the aisle she looked at every flower on ever pew, she had never seen the church look so pure. She cried the whole time and to her surprise they were happy tears. After the pastor announced that they were married Dwayne couldn't wait to go downstairs to open the gifts. She walked towards her dad and saw that he was holding a piece of paper.

"Angel now that you are married could you please sign these papers because once you are married I no longer have to pay child support and it would really help me out" he said handing her the papers.

"Your kidding right, you pay ten dollars a month, and on my wedding day instead of giving me a hug and telling me that you are here for me, you can't wait for me to cut the strings that bind you." she threw the papers at him after signing them.

She couldn't look at her father for the rest of the reception. Angel couldn't wait to finally leave and go start her life as a married woman. They had a hotel room at the Shalimar Inn for the night that her mom paid for as a gift, she felt so grown up. Dwayne carried Angel over the thresh hold. She believed that night was going to be magical and romantic. She wanted to make love to her new husband and again he turned her down. He claimed that he didn't want to hurt the baby, but they both knew the doctor had said that as long as they were careful it would be alright.

As they were snuggling on the bed there was a knock at the door, when Angel opened it she was shocked to see Lance and Lori standing there with their bathing suits.

"I invited them, that way we wouldn't be bored and we can party a little for our wedding" Dwayne said.

Angel was hurt; even worse she was pissed that on her wedding night, not only did he refuse to make love to her, but he thought that their wedding night would be boring and had invited people to come over. Not even two hours into her new marriage she felt neglected, disrespected and unloved.

DIAMOND 1990

Diamonds are a girls best friend

Right now you are going through the terrible twos
You just fell, got hurt, and run to me
I'll comfort you upon my knee
I'll kiss the boo boo and hope and prey
That the pain will go away
Now you look so content, I won't put you down for awhile
I'll just wait and see that beautiful little smile
I remember when you were born, your first cry
The nurse put you on my arm
I knew immediately I found my best friend
A friendship that will never end
I'm your mommy and I want the best for you
Remember you'll never have a problem, "I won't help you through"
I'll teach you to be proud and strong
I want you to be honest and true
But not to let anyone take advantage of you
If you can't think of anything nice to say
Just turn around and walk away
I have a few more things to say
But as I look down I notice your entering dream land
I'll now lay you down to rest
And always hope for the very best
Just one more word of advice
The Lord will always be there for you too
So I'll always pray
You'll let the Lord guide your way
And remember Diamond Dear
You'll never be too big, to sit upon my knee

And remember the Lord will always be here
You'll never be too old to say a prayer
Love Always
Your Mommy
P.S. Always come to me with
any problems you have, I'll
be there for the bad news as
well as the good news
please trust that I'll always
understand and help my
Little Diamond, my darling,
my best friend
BY: Lillian

Diamond Carol

AGE 17

The remaining three months of Angel's pregnancy and in the beginning of their marriage, Dwayne became more and more distant. At times he wouldn't even touch or talk to Angel for two or three days at a time. When he did talk to her it mostly was about the weight she was gaining, he would ask if the doctor mentioned anything to her about gaining too much weight. Angel knew that he didn't find her attractive so day by day she lost confidence and began to go out without makeup and even stopped dressing up. All of her friends had distant themselves from her because of Dwayne, he would laugh and make fun of her in front of them. She cleaned, brought him breakfast in bed and had his supper ready when he got home from work, everything she thought a wife should do. At times she even washed his hair.

It was a month before she was due and he was fired from his job that he had for nine months. They claimed they found him smoking pot in his car in the parking lot of his work. He yelled and cried, claiming they fired him because they didn't want to pay for Angel's medical bills when the baby was born. Years later he admitted that he had been smoking in the parking lot. For the next few weeks of him being at home, he became part of the furniture, never moving but to go to the bathroom. Angel had no choice but to go and sign up for welfare. She told herself that once she was away from home she would never draw welfare, but now she had a baby to think about.

One day while walking downtown she saw Constantine and he asked her if she could give him a ride because they needed to talk. He began to cry and then put his hand on hers.

"Angel you are so beautiful, I need to know that you are truly happy with Dwayne. I love you so much and if you tell me that you are really happy then, I need to move on and let you be. I can't see you with him I love you too much. If you give me a chance I will raise the baby as my own I promise. Give me one kiss and if you feel nothing than I will go but if you feel something than please ask me to stay" he said leaning in to kiss her.

"Constantine I do love Dwayne and I will never stop loving you, you were my first everything, but I'm married now and I need to think about my baby before myself" she said.

She kissed him and let him go, telling him that she didn't feel anything. She had never lied to him before but she had to set him free and leave him thinking that she didn't want him so he wouldn't have any regrets and could be happy. She never saw him again, because he moved to South Carolina. His brother Monroe didn't talk to her, blaming her for Constantine leaving him behind. She never forgave herself for letting him go, she should have told him that she did feel something, but it just wouldn't work out. She began day after day wanting her best friend back, even if friends are all they could ever be.

May 15th came and went, Angel was furious that she hadn't had her baby yet. The doctors didn't help her anger when they told her that if she should go two weeks over due then they would induce her labor. Finally on May 21st she began to feel nauseous, so she cleaned to keep her mind off of it. It felt like she had begun her period, the cramps came and went, she sat and began reading her book that told her everything that she needed to know about her pregnancy. Her cramps were every fifteen minutes and after two hours she told Dwayne that she knew she was in labor. On the ride to the hospital he looked like a lost puppy trying to find its way home. Calm down she told him, but cigarette after cigarette he became more nervous. Angel had to stay at the hospital because of the stress on the baby and her young age, they didn't dare send her home and they couldn't do anything for the pain until her contractions were at least five minutes apart.

Lil and Dwayne seemed to get along knowing that Angel was on the verge of kicking everyone out if they argued the slightest bit. The doctor rushed in when Angel started yelling in pain just to tell her that she wasn't even close. They checked her time and time again, and still after twenty-one hours she was only dilated six centimeters the doctor wanted to break her water to maybe hurry things along. He began to give her medication for the pain through an IV every two hours. The pain went from her stomach and into her back, it was so intense that for the following fourteen hours she rocked back and forth on her hands and knees. The last hour she could barely remember Dwayne's mother Cheryl coming in, and Lori acting as though she cared. Every muscle in her body ached. She wanted to give up as they rolled her onto her back. The pressure was unbearable and she could feel her baby ripping through her like fire torching her insides. Then the best words she heard in two days were "she's at ten centimeters time to push sweetie" they yelled. She began to push with every ounce of strength that she had. Everyone cried as the Doctors said they could feel the head and that the baby had a lot of hair. Her eyes went to a blur as the pressure from pushing them rise behind them. She pushed against the hands that were holding her legs up. She pushed over and over, then finally the doctor said she wasn't getting anywhere with pushing, the baby isn't moving down, she felt like a failure, like she couldn't even accomplish pushing her baby out into this world.

"We will have to pull the baby out with a suction instrument; your baby can't do this on its own. We also will have to cut the opening a bit so the baby can fit through" the Doctor explained.

She felt her private burning as they cut between her legs making way for her baby.

"We can see the head clearly now Angel, there will be a little pressure, here comes the shoulders" he said.

She looked over into Dwayne's eyes and noticed he was about to faint, then with her next glance she noticed Dwayne lying on the floor. He came to just in time to see his baby girl being born.

"It's a girl honey we have a girl and she's beautiful" Dwayne cried.

She cried so loud, it was the most beautiful sound Angel had ever heard. They laid her in her arms and she stopped crying as if she knew she was safe with her Mommy and she would never let anyone harm her. Her eyes were Angels eyes, her lips were Angel's lips and she looked into Angel's soul with those big, beautiful, brown eyes. Angel was in labor for 36 agonizing hours but when Angel felt her baby's sweet breath on her chest, all memory of pain was forgotten. On May 22, 1990 their little girl was born and they named her Diamond Carol, the old saying is diamonds are a girl's best friend, also diamonds are forever, and Angel knew that she had found her best friend forever.

Angel didn't understand how she could love someone that she had just met so much, she loved her more than life itself. She never believed in love at first sight before that moment. She was a perfect "ten" the doctor said, Angel had no doubts, but she had to stay in the hospital for four more days.

Angel had lost alot of blood and every time she stood up she fainted. So many people came to see her, it was as if she was a movie star and would only be in town for these couple of days. Angel called her Dad and he said that Katrina was sick and he would come down and see them when she got home from the hospital. Angel made herself believe that maybe her Dad didn't come down because he couldn't see her in the hospital and in pain. How could he not want to see his first grandchild she wondered?

Angel finally was released from the hospital and she watched as Dwayne became acquainted with his baby girl, he was in love. He was so gentle and at times Angel would have to beg him in order to be able to hold her own daughter. It was as if he was about to pick up a breakable piece of glass, like she was the most fragile thing in the world.

Angel wanted to be happy to see the love in his eyes and to trust him with his daughter, but something in her couldn't trust him to be alone with her. Angel stood outside the door each time Dwayne went into Diamonds room waiting to hear her cry from his touch. At times it would make Angel sick when she had the thoughts that maybe he might touch Diamond in the same way Leon touched her. Knowing that she wasn't his biological daughter he might take that out on her the way Leon had on her. Angel was up day and night for weeks waiting for the moment that she would catch him doing something to their baby girl. She would sneak home early from shopping just to find him making her laugh or smile with the slightest touch. She was the only one to give her baths and change her diapers, and she would get mad if she was gone too long and he had changed her. He would ask why, but she couldn't tell him the reason.

Dwayne's parents began to ask them when they would be moving out. They began looking and welfare was willing to help pay a security deposit if they found something. Dwayne still didn't have a job and being home everyday made him nuts. He began to fight with his brother, because Lance would hit Lori and beat on her and Dwayne wasn't having it in front of his mom and dad. Angel and Dwayne finally found a little place on Parrot Street owned by the same landlord Angels mom had in the court yard. It was a beat up place with roaches; the first floor had windows no taller than two feet from the ground, wallpaper that had seen its better days twenty years back, two bedrooms and no kitchen. There was a shower that reminded Angel of the one Leon pushed her in, but it was their place and the only one they could find. Two weeks after moving in, Lil moved all of her stuff out of Leons and moved up stairs from Angel, she felt safe with them close to her. Angel agreed to watch Alex while her mom went to work and Summer was ten by then and loved to help Angel with Diamond every moment.

Dwayne and Angel began to fight a lot about everything. They had no money because he was still unemployed and for some reason he always made it out to be Angels fault. He thought he was too good to help out around the house even when Angel went back to work. It was as if she had two children. He would leave food everywhere, and pick on Alex as if he was his age. He would take pleasure in calling him names or taunting him until Alex would hit him and then Dwayne would run to Angel so she would scold Alex and put him in the corner. She still treated Alex as her son, he was only three years older than Diamond, Dwayne hated that she treated him as well as their own daughter. Alex for some reason loved Dwayne, because that was his only male role model and Angel hated the fact that this may make him turn out to be mean like Dwayne.

The following months Dwayne refused to touch Angel in any way showing her only negative attention. Telling her that he wasn't in the mood or didn't have the time to bother with making love. Angel realized that sex wasn't everything to a marriage but she believed married couples should give their soles to one another while making love. With her back-ground, having sex became a bad habit she needed; her insides would ache if going too long without it. She wanted Dwayne to need her way she needed him, begging only led him to call her names and yell at her all the time.

Angel realized that sometimes she began to sound like her mother begging Leon to change for the sake of their child. She couldn't let Diamond grow up without a dad the way she did, blaming her for leaving her dad the way Angel still blamed her mom for leaving hers. It was a losing battle.

Dawson began to come around and he wanted to see Diamond, he believed that she still might be his. He begged Angel to let him hold her just once to see if there were any bond between them. Angel hesitated for awhile, but finally said yes, she sat watching him while he looked at Diamond with nothing but love. They looked alike, she had dark skin like his and the end of her nose wasn't round like Angels but flat like his. This made her wonder maybe Diamond was Dawson's and not that bastards! Could it be? Did the Lord grant her wish and Diamonds blood was pure not tainted with Leon's. Dwayne found out that Dawson was able to hold her and he threw one of his biggest tantrums of all he forbid Angel to ever have contact with Dawson again. It pained Angel to tell Dawson that he couldn't see her again for the sake of her marriage.

One night there was a thunderous rain storm, yet Diamond slept through it, Angel put the baby monitor in her room so she would hear her cry if she got scared of the lightning. She looked over when she heard a man's voice coming from the monitor, but Dwayne was sound asleep beside her. Frightened, she tried to wake him; he rolled over and growled at her. She tip toed through the living room stopping at Diamonds bedroom door and listened, the voice she heard was Dawson's, and he had snuck into Diamond's room and was talking to her as if she was able to understand every word he said. Angel waited knowing that he would never hurt her, she listened as he whispered I love you over and over and apologizing for not being around to see her, then there was silence and Angel thought he had left. Angel entered the room to check on Diamond, she was not in her crib. He had taken her baby out the window. She too went out the window hoping to find them but they were nowhere in sight. She ran upstairs to use Lil's phone to call the police hers had been disconnected for non payment. As she entered her mother's door she saw Dawson rocking Diamond in the chair. She was so mad, yet relieved that her thoughts were all wrong; he had missed Diamond so much that he needed to see her. They sat and talked, Angel agreed that if he never did this again, she would give him every chance to see Diamond without Dwayne knowing. Angel knew when she felt the time was right she would have to tell Dawson who Diamond's real father was.

All Down Hill

Age 18

Things with Leon had been put on hold from the courts. Day after day the attorneys would call Angel and get her hopes up telling her that they would finally be going to court, and then the next day they would call and say that it had been cancelled. They gave many different reasons for the cancellations, for example, Leon fired his lawyer again, or the judge stepped down from the case for personal reasons unknown to anyone. Meanwhile this made Leon think he had the upper hand and made Angel think he was right. What he didn't know was that this gave Angel and her attorney time to look and find more evidence against him. Angel wanted the judge to hear it all, but because it was now twelve years from the day he started touching Angel the judge advised her that she couldn't tell everything. Angel was aware that the jury would get an ear full of just the things he had done to her between the ages of twelve and sixteen, but she still wanted them to hear about the beginning.

Meanwhile Angel just sat and waited for the court dates to come and go. Leon had his people follow her and he himself would ride up and down her street several times a day. On one particular hot day Angel and her family were sitting outside her apartment and she noticed his truck coming up the street "I'm not going to run" she told herself, "I'm not going to let him know that I am afraid as hell of him". He stopped in front of her and stared at Diamond, then smiled at Angel, she got up and ran into the house and he now knew that still she was afraid, she was not afraid for herself but for her daughter. After that she watched out the windows and waited before she stepped outside to make sure that it was clear. Day after day of watching him drive by Angel realized that he hadn't even touched Diamond and she was already in his grip, not being able to get Diamond out of her carriage until she covered her with a blanket so if Leon was around he could not see her.

Again the families were all sitting outside and sure enough there comes his truck around the corner and Angel carried Diamond inside fast, she yelled to her Mom who was on the other side of the road to get Alex and Summer inside the house also. Leon stopped in front of the house, fearful, Lil stood still and then made her way towards the truck. Angel stood on the other side listening hoping to hear it all.

"Lil you know all of this is foolishness. I have never touched that girl she wants you and Brad to get back together and that is why she's doing this. Here is some money for Summer and Alex" he said.

Alex saw his truck from inside the house and came running out and ran towards the truck. Lil just stood frozen with fear as Leon opened the door and grabbed Alex.

"Now what are you going to do" he yelled as he drove off.

Angel went to call the police and Lil begged her not to she explained if Angel called the police then he would hurt Alex. Lil pleaded with her to please let her go and talk to him and then he will give him back. She got in her car and drove off. All that went through Angels mind was the pain he could give them and within thirty minutes the phone rang it was Lil saying everything was ok. Hours later she was home with Alex and Angel tried to get her to tell her what he made her do to get him back.

"Angel if you don't drop this whole thing I will see all of you at your funerals" as she told Angel this she looked as though she already saw them dead. Angel knew that this robotic move from Lil was Leons grip on her.

The next day they went to court and told her lawyer what had happened to Alex. Justice was partially served and the judge told them that Leon was a threat and he now would be held without bail until the court date.

While Angel concentrated on court at home Dwayne became meaner, leaving for nights at a time and still had no job so the fighting only became worse. Angel went out and within two days she had a job and told him that he would have to watch Diamond. He assured her that he would continue to look for a job and keep her safe from Leon's family. Angel of course believed his lies and every day when she came home he went out and in an hour or two complained that there wasn't any work out there. Angel yelled about seeing all the help wanted signs up, he then came back to not wanted to work in places that his friends would make fun of him. He began to hang out with trouble makers around the neighbor hood. He began to smoke pot and Angel would come home to Diamond screaming and him

lying on the couch high and unable to move. As Angel screamed time and time again about his behavior he would play his mind games and talk her into believing that it was somehow her fault for his unemployment.

It was 4 pm the night of her eighteenth birthday and Dwayne had a party planned for her but first they had to go to Henry's. Lil watched Diamond, and then Angel and Dwayne walked to Henry's, Angel had high hopes that he had somehow changed, but he left her to go to the store and get her some wine coolers. Hours went by and there still was no sign of Dwayne or Henry. Angel finally was fed up and began to walk home, she realized as she walked through the door it was already eleven at night. She couldn't go to sleep not knowing what he was up to, she got up and dressed and went to look for him. She knew that no excuse would be good enough this time. Angel went door to door, store to store but no one had seen him.

As she continued to ask people if they had seen her husband Angel realized that this must have been how her mom felt looking for her dad all those times. She finally was about to give up when she stopped at a local pizza place to get a drink. She described to the waitress what Dwayne and Henry looked like hoping she might have seen them.

"Yes they were in here earlier and they invited me to a party that they were going to but I had to work. They gave me this number to call if I wanted to see them again." she said showing Angel a paper with Angels own number on it.

Angel walked home and the more she walked the madder she became. He finally showed up staggering in the door at three in the morning. Before Angel could say anything he jumped at her blaming Henry for them not getting home. Angel lashed out telling him that she wanted a divorce, she knew that she couldn't take it anymore. He grabbed her and held her against the wall yelling into her face and his grip became harder hurting her arms.

"You're not going anywhere until we talk this out" he yelled.

"Let me go your hurting me, please let go, now let go" she begged as she pictured Leon holding her still.

She picked up the first thing she could grab, a pan, and hit him with it just so he would let go. He fell to the ground, she had knocked him out she realized as she looked at him that this might have been extreme, but when you're in a situation and can't think of a way out you do what you have to she thought. As she ran to the phone to call the police Dwayne came to and hugged her after seeing the fear in her eyes.

The following day they talked things out and he begged for another chance. They both agreed that they had to move away from the crowds and drugs. Leon claimed that the reason why he did the things that he did was because Lil was always in their business and this stressed him out. Thinking that a move might solve their problems, they found an apartment a half a mile away on Homestead Street. In the apartment below was her Aunt Anne, so she felt relieved that she had someone to talk to when things became bad again.

Their apartment was huge, three big bedrooms and a small back room off of the master bedroom. Angel loved her new apartment and worked day and night to fix it up. She made a special room in the back for Dwayne's tattooing dream. One week later Lil moved across the street, she felt safe as long as she was near Angel. This made Dwayne irate he wanted to get away from the family and now they followed. After only one month of living on the hill Angel knew that they couldn't stay for long because this was the same hill as where her molestation began with Leon, but again she wanted to face her fears as Dwayne said and what better way to do this then stare them down.

To Angels surprise, with the move Dwayne seemed different and he became a perfect dad and husband. They discussed it and after a few months they knew that they wanted another baby, Diamond was two already and she needed a sibling. Not long after trying Angel became pregnant; Angel was convinced that the Lord was giving them a new beginning. In turn she promised the Lord that she would try to keep her marriage together and happy.

Only three months into her pregnancy and Dwayne started using his old excuses not to touch her. Angel of course had her doubts about him cheating. He claimed time and time again that he wouldn't cheat.

Her answers to his cheating finally came to a close when she went to develop film, pictures she had taken of Diamond at the park. She was shocked when she opened the package and the second picture she saw was a naked lady in her bath tub and holding one of the ladies breasts was a hand and if it wasn't for the tattoo on his arm then maybe he would have a chance to deny it. Angel looked closer and noticed that it was the same lady Dwayne was flirting with at the carnival two nights before. When Angel confronted him about it he lied like always and said that they were just kidding around, his friend John was even there and they wanted to play a trick on Angel. He was pissed when Angel talked to John before he did and John said he didn't know anything about it. Angel started to hyperventilate and became nauseous and worried about the baby so she dropped the whole thing.

The sickness stayed for days and after seeing the doctor he ordered an ultrasound, because the complications that she had had with her pregnancy with Diamond. Before even starting the test the nurse asked all sorts of questions. The main one was whether she had felt the baby move yet. "She hadn't felt it yet" she answered.

"Did we hear a heart beat at your last examination" the nurse asked.

"Yes" Angel said.

They then began the test first applying the hot gel over her belly, and then moving the instrument back and forth and up and down the length of her belly. She became more and more nervous remembering how they could hear Diamonds heart beat right away and she didn't hear anything this time. The monitor screen was pointed her way and she could see her baby on it curled into the usual fetal position. The nurse stood up and excused herself from the room and then returned with the doctor.

"Angel and Dwayne I have some bad news" he moved the instrument around just as the nurse did moments before.

"Please tell me I don't care how bad it is I just need to know if my baby is alright or not" she cried knowing that something was terribly wrong just by the looks on their faces.

"I'm so sorry but your baby's heart stopped and it appears as if the baby never went past the two month stage, it didn't continue to grow at all" he said.

"Why would it just stop and what do we do now" crying and remembering Francis and how no one had an explanation on why her heart just stopped.

"We will need to do a DNC this is a one day surgery we will go in and remove the fetus and your recovery will be very short. Now this doesn't mean that you won't be able to have another baby in the future, you will want to wait at least three months before trying again" he said this with such ease acting as though Angel would get over losing her baby in just moments after the surgery.

The following day Angel was at the hospital at six am sharp, they put an IV in and rolled her into the operating room immediately. The dead air she breathed in, the coldness engulfing her body as she lay on a metal slab. They put a mask over her mouth and nose and told her to count back from one hundred. She remembers counting to ninety-seven and the room got dark. She woke up in the same room where it all began. Dwayne and her mom stood over her looking as though they had just entered a funeral and didn't know what to say, but "sorry".

"The doctor said that the surgery went as planned and that you should be better in a couple of days" Dwayne said as he held her hand and leaned in for a kiss.

"Don't touch me please, don't you realize that this happened because we fight all the damn time, we put the baby in so much stress that they just had to scrap the baby out of me like it was nothing to begin with" Angel said pushing his hand away from her face. She realized as she rubbed her belly that it had now been emptied of the baby she wanted so badly.

When they got home she walked up the stairs and into the empty room that was going to be the nursery. She sat in the rocking chair that her mom gave her after Diamond was born and held the bear that would be sitting in the babies crib just months away. She cried and cried feeling as though it must have been a bad dream and any minute she would wake and feel her baby move.

A month went by and the Doctor confirmed that she healed very well and she could try again to get pregnant in only two short months. Only time would tell.

Freedom

Angel finally went to her last appointment with Barbara; she claimed that this was it, no more continuances for court, the judge was fed up. As she sat in her chair one last time she felt relieved and scared at the same time.

"Some bad news Angel, because you can't remember all the dates and some court technicalities. We can only get him charged with the dates you can remember" she said as she handed Angel a piece of paper with only five counts against him.

All the charges were past the age twelve. Angel's heart sank as she read the paper and realized that no matter the pain he had caused her because of her memory, because of dates that she couldn't remember he was getting away with almost everything. She was so mad that she threw the paper back at Barbara.

"You mean everything he has done to me from the age of six and all the things he has done to mom and the animals don't matter" she said wishing she had told her about the shower and more detail about the cottage.

"It all matters but unfortunately we can't prove it. You can however, tell your whole story, but unfortunately only so many charges will be brought against him. I will be with you the whole time just look at me in the court room. Answer only the questions they ask! Sometimes they will stand behind Leon knowing that you will automatically look toward them when answering their questions. They will try to intimidate you by reducing eye contact. Just keep looking at me and answer their questions the best way you know how" she said.

"It's very hard for me to look at someone else when I am talking to another" Angel explained; thinking this was the worst thing they could do.

"Also, they are going to ask you about the other people you have had sex with. I have to tell you Angel they did question Robert about having sex with you everyday or so and they measured his penis to see if it was as big as you said it was, but don't worry he was very proud of that and admitted to having sex with you a lot. Remember it is ok to cry it will show them how much he hurt you" she continued.

"You don't understand, it's hard for me to cry in front of him, that is one thing I never let him see was how much he hurt me" she said laughing inside while she imagined Robert standing there with his dick in a cops hand and being proud of its enormous size.

In just hours they would be led into a court room full of people, some of who Angel knew and some she has never seen before. As Angel walked into the court room she recognized the back of Leon's head, panic washed over her, leaving her frozen with fear, no need for her to look for a familiar, comforting face, she already knew her family would not be there because they may be called as witnesses. Never had she felt so alone! She walked down the middle of the court room she thought for a moment that she had smelt his scent linger in the air and to her left seated were his family members, his mother shot an empty, yet evil glare her way. She sat in the chair that they had practiced in just days before. Everybody rose as the judge walked in and took his seat. Then all took their assigned seats. Twelve jurors entered and took their seats. Angel looked at them all, her eyes scanning the room to find a friendly face, just as Barbara had told her to, one that she could tell her story to.

After their opening arguments Leons lawyer sat down and nodded as Angels Lawyer Elaine stayed standing. The following forms are from the District Court where the trial was held.

The State of New Hampshire

KNAP
_____ COUNTY

SUPERIOR COURT

STATE PRISON SENTENCE

a/Verdict: __GUILTY BY JURY__   State v. _____

rk: _____   Docket # __5-92-032__

no: _____   Crime: __AGG. FELONIOUS SEXUAL ASSAULT__

ge: _____   Date of Crime: _____

A finding of GUILTY is entered.

[X] The defendant is sentenced to the New Hampshire State Prison for not more than __15__ year(s) (months), nor less than __7 1/2__ year(s) (months). There is added to the minimum sentence a disciplinary period equal to 150 days for each year of the minimum term of the defendant's sentence, to be prorated for any part of the year.

[ ] This sentence is to be served as follows:
   [ ] Stand committed   [ ] Commencing _____

[ ] _____ of the minimum sentence is suspended;
   _____ of the maximum sentence is suspended.
   Suspensions are conditioned upon good behavior and compliance with all of the terms of this order. Any suspended sentence may be imposed after a hearing brought by the State within _____ years of today's date.

[X] __ALL_____ of the sentence is deferred for a period of __2__ years after release on 5-92-027/028/029
   Thirty (30) days prior to the expiration of the deferred period, the defendant may petition the Court to show cause why the deferred commitment should not be imposed. Failure to petition within the prescribed time will result in imposition of the deferred commitment without further hearing.

[ ] _____ of the minimum sentence may be suspended by the Court on application of the defendant provided he demonstrates meaningful participation in a sexual offender program while incarcerated.

[X] The sentence is [X] consecutive to 5-92-027/028/029/030/031
   [ ] concurrent with _____

[ ] Pretrial confinement credit: _____ days.

[X] The Court recommends to the Department of Corrections:
   A. [ ] Drug and alcohol treatment and counseling.
   B. [X] Sexual offender program. Meaningful participation in and successful completion of
   C. [ ] Sentence to be served at the House of Corrections.
   D. [X] Meaningful participation in and continued sexual offender counseling recommend by Sexual Offender Program upon release from State Prison.

Angel Costello

RSA Ch 632-A Sec 2   Docket # S-92-028

   Class A
   [illegible]
                                   Original 2

THE STATE OF NEW HAMPSHIRE

BELKNAP, SS.

    At the Superior Court, holden at ▮▮▮, within and for the County of ▮▮▮ aforesaid on the 7TH day of JANUARY in the year of our Lord one thousand nine hundred and ninety-two

    THE GRAND JURORS FOR THE STATE OF NEW HAMPSHIRE, upon their oath, present that:

    ▮▮▮
    DOB: 12/26/49

of ROUTE 106, ▮▮▮, NH in the County of ▮▮▮ between the 11TH DAY OF APRIL, 1985 AND THE 10TH day of April in the year of our Lord one thousand nine hundred and eighty-six at ▮▮▮ in the County of ▮▮▮ aforesaid with force and arms,

    DID PURPOSELY ENGAGE IN SEXUAL PENETRATION WITH ANOTHER PERSON WHO IS LESS THAN THIRTEEN (13) YEARS OF AGE, IN THAT ▮▮▮ DID ENGAGE IN ANAL INTERCOURSE WITH A FEMALE JUVENILE WHOSE DATE OF BIRTH IS APRIL 11, 1973 (04/11/73) BY INSERTING HIS PENIS INTO THE ANUS OF SAID FEMALE JUVENILE,

contrary to the form of the Statute, in such case made and provided, and against the peace and dignity of the State.

This is a true bill

                                    County Attorney
                                   ~~Attorney General~~

      10
   Foreperson.

iA Ch 632-A Sec 2

Class A
~~~~~~~~~~~~

DOCKET # 5-92-241

original

THE STATE OF NEW HAMPSHIRE

BELKNAP. SS.

At the Superior Court, holden at ███████ within and for the
County of ███████ aforesaid on the _7TH_ day of _JANUARY_
in the year of our Lord one thousand nine hundred and ninety-two

THE GRAND JURORS FOR THE STATE OF NEW HAMPSHIRE, upon their
oath, present that:

████████

DOB: 12/26/49

of _ROUTE 106,_ ███████ _NH_ in the County of ███████ between the
11TH DAY OF APRIL, 1985 AND THE 10TH day of _April_ in the year of
our Lord one thousand nine hundred and eighty-six at ███████ in
the County of ███████ aforesaid with force and arms,

DID PURPOSELY ENGAGE IN SEXUAL PENETRATION WITH ANOTHER
PERSON WHO IS LESS THAN THIRTEEN (13) YEARS OF AGE, IN
THAT ███████ DID ENGAGE IN SEXUAL INTERCOURSE WITH
A FEMALE JUVENILE WHOSE DATE OF BIRTH IS APRIL 11, 1973
(04/11/73) BY INSERTING HIS PENIS INTO THE VAGINA OF SAID
FEMALE JUVENILE,

contrary to the form of the Statute, in such case made and
provided, and against the peace and dignity of the State.

This is a true bill.

County Attorney
~~Attorney General~~

Foreperson.

147

Angel Costello

Class A

THE STATE OF NEW HAMPSHIRE

BELKNAP, SS.

At the Superior Court, holden at ▆▆▆▆ within and for the
County of ▆▆▆▆ aforesaid on the _7TH_ day of _JANUARY_
in the year of our Lord one thousand nine hundred and ninety-two

THE GRAND JURORS FOR THE STATE OF NEW HAMPSHIRE, upon their
oath, present that:

▆▆▆

DOB: 12/26/49

of _ROUTE 106,_ ▆▆▆▆ _NH_ in the County of ▆▆▆ between the
11TH DAY OF APRIL, 1985 AND THE 10TH day of _April_ in the year of
our Lord one thousand nine hundred and eighty-six at ▆▆▆▆ in
the County of ▆▆▆ aforesaid with force and arms,

DID PURPOSELY ENGAGE IN SEXUAL PENETRATION WITH ANOTHER
PERSON WHO IS LESS THAN THIRTEEN (13) YEARS OF AGE, IN
THAT ▆▆▆ DID ENGAGE IN DIGITAL PENETRATION WITH
A FEMALE JUVENILE WHOSE DATE OF BIRTH IS APRIL 11, 1973
(04/11/73) BY INSERTING HIS FINGER INTO THE VAGINA OF
SAID FEMALE JUVENILE,

contrary to the form of the Statute, in such case made and
provided, and against the peace and dignity of the State.

This is a true bill.

Asst County Attorney
~~Attorney General~~

Foreperson.

INDICTMENT

148

Ch 632-A Sec 2

Class A
NATIONAL ONLY

Docket # S-92-030

Original A

THE STATE OF NEW HAMPSHIRE

BELKNAP. SS.

At the Superior Court, holden at ▬▬▬▬, within and for the County of ▬▬▬▬ aforesaid on the 7TH day of JANUARY in the year of our Lord one thousand nine hundred and ninety-two

THE GRAND JURORS FOR THE STATE OF NEW HAMPSHIRE, upon their oath, present that:

▬▬▬▬

DOB: 12/26/49

of ROUTE 106, ▬▬▬▬, NH in the County of ▬▬▬▬ between the 11TH DAY OF APRIL, 1984 AND THE 10TH day of April in the year of our Lord one thousand nine hundred and eighty-five at ▬▬▬ in the County of ▬▬▬▬ aforesaid with force and arms,

DID PURPOSELY ENGAGE IN SEXUAL PENETRATION WITH ANOTHER PERSON WHO IS LESS THAN THIRTEEN (13) YEARS OF AGE, IN THAT ▬▬▬ DID ENGAGE IN SEXUAL INTERCOURSE WITH A FEMALE JUVENILE WHOSE DATE OF BIRTH IS APRIL 11, 1973 (04/11/73) BY INSERTING HIS PENIS INTO THE VAGINA OF SAID FEMALE JUVENILE,

contrary to the form of the Statute, in such case made and provided, and against the peace and dignity of the State.

This is a true bill

~~Hst~~ County Attorney
~~Attorney General~~

Foreperson.

149

Ch 632-A Sec 2

Class A

~~CRIMINAL CODE~~

original 5

THE STATE OF NEW HAMPSHIRE

BELKNAP. SS.

At the Superior Court, holden at ████ within and for the County of ████ aforesaid on the _7TH_ day of _JANUARY_ in the year of our Lord one thousand nine hundred and ninety-two

THE GRAND JURORS FOR THE STATE OF NEW HAMPSHIRE, upon their oath, present that:

████

DOB: 12/26/49

of ROUTE 106, ████, NH in the County of ████ between the _11TH DAY OF APRIL, 1982 AND THE 10TH_ day of _April_ in the year of our Lord one thousand nine hundred and eighty-four at ████ in the County of ████ aforesaid with force and arms,

DID PURPOSELY ENGAGE IN SEXUAL PENETRATION WITH ANOTHER PERSON WHO IS LESS THAN THIRTEEN (13) YEARS OF AGE, IN THAT ████ DID ENGAGE IN CUNNILINGUS WITH A FEMALE JUVENILE WHOSE DATE OF BIRTH IS APRIL 11, 1973 (04/11/73) BY PLACING HIS TONGUE ON THE VAGINA OF SAID FEMALE JUVENILE,

contrary to the form of the Statute, in such case made and provided, and against the peace and dignity of the State.

This is a true bill.

Asst County Attorney ~~Attorney General~~

Foreperson,

Class A
official only

origenals .92.03½
·½·

THE STATE OF NEW HAMPSHIRE

BELKNAP, SS.

At the Superior Court, holden at ████████, within and for the County of ████████ aforesaid on the <u>7TH</u> day of <u>JANUARY</u> in the year of our Lord one thousand nine hundred and ninety-two

THE GRAND JURORS FOR THE STATE OF NEW HAMPSHIRE, upon their oath, present that:

████

DOB: 12/26/49

of <u>ROUTE 106,</u> ████████, <u>NH</u> in the County of ████████ between the <u>11TH DAY OF APRIL, 1981 AND THE 10TH</u> day of <u>April</u> in the year of our Lord one thousand nine hundred and eighty-two at ████████ in the County of ████ aforesaid with force and arms,

DID PURPOSELY ENGAGE IN SEXUAL PENETRATION WITH ANOTHER PERSON WHO IS LESS THAN THIRTEEN (13) YEARS OF AGE, IN THAT ████████ DID ENGAGE IN DIGITAL PENETRATION WITH A FEMALE JUVENILE WHOSE DATE OF BIRTH IS APRIL 11, 1973 (04/11/73) BY INSERTING HIS FINGER INTO THE VAGINA OF SAID FEMALE JUVENILE,

contrary to the form of the Statute, in such case made and provided, and against the peace and dignity of the State.

This is a true bill.

County Attorney
~~Attorney General~~

Foreperson.

INDICTMENT

151

Angel Costello

Class A
NATIONAL ONLY

S-92-033
Original-T

THE STATE OF NEW HAMPSHIRE

BELKNAP, SS.

At the Superior Court, holden at ███████, within and for the County of ███████ aforesaid on the 7TH day of JANUARY in the year of our Lord one thousand nine hundred and ninety-two

THE GRAND JURORS FOR THE STATE OF NEW HAMPSHIRE, upon their oath, present that:

███████
DOB: 12/25/49

of ROUTE 106, ███████, NH in the County of ███████ between the 11TH DAY OF APRIL, 1983 AND THE 10TH day of April in the year of our Lord one thousand nine hundred and eighty-five at ███████ in the County of ███████ aforesaid with force and arms,

DID PURPOSELY ENGAGE IN SEXUAL PENETRATION WITH ANOTHER PERSON WHO IS LESS THAN THIRTEEN (13) YEARS OF AGE, IN THAT ███████ DID ENGAGE IN SEXUAL INTERCOURSE WITH A FEMALE JUVENILE WHOSE DATE OF BIRTH IS APRIL 11, 1973 (04/11/73) BY INSERTING HIS PENIS INTO THE VAGINA OF SAID FEMALE JUVENILE,

contrary to the form of the Statute, in such case made and provided, and against the peace and dignity of the State.

This is a true bill.

Asst County Attorney
~~Attorney General~~

Foreperson.

INDICTMENT

152

Ch 632-A Sec 2   Docket # S-92-03¼
  Class A
~~~~~~~~ ~~~~

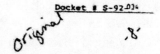

THE STATE OF NEW HAMPSHIRE

BELKNAP, SS.

    At the Superior Court, holden at ████████ within and for the
County of ████████ aforesaid on the <u>7TH</u> day of <u>JANUARY</u>
in the year of our Lord one thousand nine hundred and ninety-two

    THE GRAND JURORS FOR THE STATE OF NEW HAMPSHIRE, upon their
oath, present that:

                 ████████

                 DOB: 12/26/49

of <u>ROUTE 106,</u> ████████, <u>NH</u> in the County of ████████ between the
<u>11TH DAY OF APRIL, 1983 AND THE 10TH</u> day of <u>April</u> in the year of
our Lord one thousand nine hundred and eighty-five at ████████ in
the County of ████████ aforesaid with force and arms,

    DID PURPOSELY ENGAGE IN SEXUAL PENETRATION WITH ANOTHER
PERSON WHO IS LESS THAN THIRTEEN (13) YEARS OF AGE, IN
THAT ████████ DID ENGAGE IN DIGITAL PENETRATION WITH
A FEMALE JUVENILE WHOSE DATE OF BIRTH IS APRIL 11, 1973
(04/11/73) BY INSERTING HIS FINGER INTO THE VAGINA OF
SAID FEMALE JUVENILE,

contrary to the form of the Statute, in such case made and
provided, and against the peace and dignity of the State.

This is a true bill.

                                    Asst County Attorney
                                   ~~Attorney General~~

                Foreperson.

After the court hearing was all over Angel went to her dad's house and away from everyone. While at her dads Barbara called her to let her know the news that she can finally start the life she should have had years ago.

"Angel, Leon received 17-34 years in prison. You are finally free" she yelled over the phone.

Angel held Diamond so close as she cried in hysterics. She shouted "We are free he's finally gone". It was as if she had been in a torture chamber for years and someone finally opened the door and let her out. She could see the people around her clearer than ever before. As if for all those years she had, a blind fold on only seeing shadows walking in front of her. She called her mom and by the sound of her cheers she had already heard the news. She yelled from the depths of her soul "WE ARE FREE ANGEL, WE ARE FREE".

For the following months Dwayne and Angel regained their love that was for almost a year put on hold. He treated her like a queen and she treated him like a king. Everyone around them admired their relationship and he began to want her again.

This made her wonder what if all the times they had fought was her fault, maybe she started it all. She was too involved in Leon to pay attention to this wonderful man standing right in front of her. She was free to fall in love, finally.

Another Try

"Honey let's try again for another baby. The doctor said to wait awhile and we have waited. Diamond deserves to have a baby brother or sister" Dwayne asked.

"Ok but please promise me that things will stay the same as they have. I love the way we are right now" she begged.

It was that easy one month later Angel was pregnant again. The family was happy about the news, Aunt Ann prayed for them and for the first time in a long time Angel went to church hoping that being in the Lords house she would be blessed with a healthy baby. Angel began to show very quickly and the doctor said that everything was going great. He scheduled an ultrasound when she was three months along.

Angel lay there just as before but this time she didn't look at the screen. Dwayne squeezed her hand as they heard the most wonderful sound, their baby's heart beat. "It's ok to look honey, our baby is moving" Dwayne said. Angel slowly turned her head to see for herself and there was this beautiful image on the screen.

"You two should know that the heart beat isn't as strong as we want it to be, but just stay stress free and stay rested. We will schedule you for another ultrasound next month just to keep things going" the Dr. said.

The month seemed to drag on and on as she waited for her appointment. The following month she went to the Doctors office and again the ultrasound showed a healthy baby and the heart beat sounded strong. That same day they went and told the family that the baby was doing just great. Angel went shopping and bought a few things positive that her baby would be ok. For being so young Diamond seemed to know what was going on and brought in one of her baby bunnies and put in into the rocking chair then said "baby" as she pushed it back.

Diamond was so smart being only two she said full sentences and was aware of everything. She began to walk at just nine months. At eleven months she began to run around and take her clothes off Angel found that as the perfect opportunity to potty train. They went out and bought her a potty chair and it took just once showing her what to do then she trained herself.

Another ultrasound just two months after the second one was scheduled and Dwayne said he would go with Angel every time. Angel knew the routine and lay on the bed lifting up her shirt and realized how small the instrument was that could seal her baby's future into this world. This time the Doctor chose to do the ultrasound himself, this helped Angel relax a little bit more.

"OK Angel a bit of pressure" he said moving the wand across her belly side to side. Angel winced as the doctor put pressure on her full bladder.

The room went silent hearing nothing but the tick tock of the clock above them. Angel watched Dwayne's face and noticed tears running down his cheeks.

"Sorry Angel" the doctor said and knowing somehow there wasn't any need to explain.

Angel began to cry and felt as though someone reached into her chest and yanked her heart out. Dwayne held her hand and knew that this time they had done everything they could to reassure the baby's health, then Angel thought of all that she would have to go through again with the surgery, the crying and hoping that she might someday have another baby. As the surgery was scheduled for the very next day, Dwayne continued to tell Angel that he knew what she was going through but he hadn't had a clue. He didn't feel the movement of another life inside him. To feel a life at one moment and to have your body attach itself to another living being and then to know that your insides have died.

"Do you want me to go and get Diamond that way you can see her when you're done" Dwayne asked in the hopes that seeing her baby girl might help her from thinking about her baby being dragged out of her.

"No I don't want her to see me this way" Angel said as the nurse came to get her and bring her into the operating room.

What seemed like minutes it was all over and there she lay waiting to go home to another empty nursery? Dwayne wasn't there and the nurse gave her a message saying he had to go to work his boss called him in.

He was now working for a private business installing floors; Angel had a feeling that those floors could wait until after the surgery and she was back home. Just as she began to cry thinking she would be stranded in that hospital till later that night explaining why her husband wasn't there to get her. She looked up and noticed some friendly faces. It was Lil, Alex and Diamond walking towards her.

It seemed to be so dark before they came in, their smiles lit the place up. Lil waved to her as if she hadn't seen her in months and Diamond continued pulling on Alex in hopes he would let go of her hand so she could run to Angel. She thought back and wondered why she ever told Dwayne she didn't want to see her baby girl when seeing her felt just right. Diamond finally broke free and ran and climbed into bed with her mom, and then Angel looked for Alex and couldn't find him, then she noticed he was hiding behind Lil.

"Come here, come and see sis" Angel called out to him extending her hand.

"No" he said growling.

"I have something for you" holding her hand behind her acting as if she had a gift for him. He walked towards her putting his hand out. She pulled him to her and gave him the biggest kiss and hug. He just hugged her and didn't want to let go and she didn't want him to.

"Mom" Alex said as he pulled his mom towards him and tried to whisper.

Alex has really bad hearing and when he thinks he's whispering he really is talking loud enough for people around him to hear.

"What honey" Lil answered.

"Can you please give my sissy a baby boy, because God won't let her have one" he said in his tiniest voice.

Angel hugged him and cried and reassured him that God will give her a baby one of these days when God thinks she's ready to have one.

"Alex don't you know that you are the only boy that sissy needs. You are the only boy in my life that still makes me laugh and makes my heart fill up with joy. It's because of those pudgy cheeks of yours and that gorgeous smile" Angel said and he gave her a smile.

They went home and Angel was still very upset that Dwayne's choice was to go to work. She wanted to stay mad to let him know how much he hurt her. Then while she lay in bed he brought her in the biggest dinner and of course she forgave him seeing all the work he put into it.

"I have been thinking about our marriage lately and think its time to spice it up. I was wondering if you would be willing to have a threesome with another girl" he asked.

Angel felt as though she should have known better, he never did anything nice unless he was going to get something out of it. She couldn't believe that he would ask her this on the very day she lost another baby. She laughed and laughed at him asking that maybe he could let her heal from just having her insides just about ripped out. Then after she was healed she would think about it and he could ask her again.

She couldn't help but think about that question for the next two weeks. Maybe this was why he didn't make love to her; maybe she wasn't enough for him. As a wife you think of different ways to please your husband; think of ways to make him happy. She tried to spice things up over the next couple of months, everything from lap dancing, stripping for him, and even letting him screw her in the ass like he always wanted to. Being in pain for days after, in hopes that now he would be happy. But all these things didn't matter every time he would get drunk he would still persist that he needed to see her with another woman. He even told her that she could choose the other woman herself that way she would feel comfortable. If only he knew that her fears weren't him leaving her for the other woman it was, that in doing this she may prove to herself that she needed a woman. What would happen to her family, her husband, her little girl, what would happen if she needed this other woman more that she needed Dwayne?

The day finally came and after him begging her day after day, she went over to Arlene's house she knew that she could trust her with Dwayne and her being a good friend she wouldn't want to mess that up by falling for her. Angel asked her and without hesitation she said yes, telling her that she always wanted to try to be with another girl. She had one condition that they would sleep together before doing it in front of Dwayne that way she could tell her if she did anything wrong. They planned it and one day she came over they decided to sleep with each other before Dwayne came home from work.

Angel went home and lit candles making it as comfortable for Arlene as possible. As she heard her footsteps coming up the stairs she threw on a naughty nightie and a robe. Arlene knocked on the door before going in and Angel took her hand and led her to the bedroom asking her again if she was sure she wanted to do this. Angel could only notice how gorgeous she looked with her hair up in a bun and she was wearing no makeup which made her more beautiful, if possible. Arlene reassured Angel with a kiss that she was sure. They walked into the bedroom and Arlene's eyes lit up when she saw all the candles, she looked radiant as the candles reflected off her dark skin and then she let her hair down. The curls fell to the middle of her back. Angel could feel the nervousness as she undressed her.

"Ok so here I am sexy as ever, do what you will to me" she said wiggling her ass and turning around and around showing Angel her naked body.

They caressed one another and began to caress each other everywhere. It felt as though they had done it time and time again, it certainly didn't feel like their first time being together. Angel realized as she lay on top of Arlene how soft her body was and in her heart she knew this was what she had been missing all this time. Just as Angel was mesmerized by how wonderful it felt to have another woman with her the door opened slowly and to both of their surprise there stood Dwayne. Angel wanted him to leave so she could finish, she wanted Arlene to herself. Then Arlene motioned for him to come and join them, this made Angel angry but she surrendered. He got undressed and jumped into bed acting like a boy in the candy store. Angel felt left out and she got up as they continued to fuck and they didn't even notice when she left. They stayed in there for another hour and Arlene came out and kissed Angel before leaving. Dwayne walked out and thanked Angel for finally putting a smile on his face and it was funny because all she had to do was leave to make him smile.

She thought that this would have brought them even closer but for some reason it pushed them apart. Dwayne began to push Angel away even when all she would want was a simple kiss in the morning before leaving. This went on for months and she began to look around for people who would show her attention. The attention that she wanted came, but not in a person she had expected it to come from, the man that gave this to her was one of her oldest girl friends man, Meredith's man Alvin. Angel still had all this built up hatred towards Meredith for not coming to her wedding. Angel cheated on Dwayne and felt terrible for doing it but it was as if she couldn't help herself. She was in need of sex, anyone would have done but it had to be someone who didn't want anything else from her but sex.

Dwayne began to flirt with everyone right in front of Angel and tried his damnest to make her feel like trash. He would say things like "nobody would want you, you are fat, ugly and already have a kid" this only made her go out to prove to herself that men wanted her. She began to see herself as fat; being only 130 pounds, and ugly she began to dress up only to cheat. Dwayne began to cheat then she would cheat, it became a game to them.

Finally their anniversary came around and Angel thought maybe they should start over again she lit the candles, made dinner and felt foolish when he never came home. Leaving her there to celebrate by herself drowning in her own self pity. He finally staggered in at four in the morning and climbed into bed. She thought maybe he had just forgotten and if that was the case they will celebrate it the following night. Then he slapped her ass and asked how their anniversary went.

"You remembered it was our anniversary and you didn't even bother to come home, then you have the nerve to ask me how our anniversary went" she asked.

"Well I'll tell you my anniversary went great, I know I'm a little drunk why don't you start celebrating by giving me head" he said laughing.

The following month Angel found out that she was pregnant again. Dwayne acted as though he was proud. Angel sat him down and asked him "how in the world could you think that this baby was yours when we haven't had sex in months". Out of the cheating game they played, she became pregnant. He chose to forgive her and wanted to stay and raise the baby as his own. How could she say no, she knew the baby belonged to someone else but she still thought she could make her marriage work?

They went for an ultrasound again and she was in fact pregnant with twins. She was afraid but thought Alvin should know about them. Alvin agreed that the best thing would be to let everyone think that the babies belonged to Dwayne. Angel still had some weight on from the last baby so she knew that she could wait for a bit before telling the family. That didn't last but two months and she ballooned only around the stomach, so everyone had to know. They all began to ask Dwayne about her being pregnant and this started to make him mad. He knew these babies didn't belong to him and so he started a huge fight one night. He blamed all the cheating on Angel claiming that maybe none of the babies belonged to him. He thought maybe she became pregnant from other guys and let him think they were his in hopes to save their marriage. That fight ended up with Angel in the hospital having a miscarriage. Angel threatened to divorce him letting him know that she couldn't take the fighting anymore.

This led to breakfast in bed everyday and roses on the table at night. They were happy for awhile and decided that she wouldn't have another baby, that maybe the stress of pregnancy was what was wrong in their marriage.

The Split Up

AGE 19

As the months passed, the arguments between Angel and Dwayne became less frequent. Dwayne became the father and husband Angel had always wanted him to be. The love they shared seemed to be stronger than ever.

There was a new man in Lil's life, his name was Jeremy. Lil as always rushed things and moved in with him and his two little girls, Ainsley who was nine, (same age as Summer) and Kendall who was seven. Although Angel was happy for her mom, she was unable to trust anyone with her younger sister and brother, because of Leon. She knew she had to check things out in order to protect Summer and Alex if need be. Angel was sure of one thing, that Ainsley was the dominate one and in control of Kendall. She feared this conduct would carry over to include her siblings.

Lil knew that Jeremy wasn't the best father to his girls. He was a kind man, yet irresponsible, he needed someone to take control and make decisions for him. Lil could see that his girls paid for this because they were out of control, but she felt that maybe with time she could change things.

Angel noticed that Ainsley would hurt Kendall every chance she got, and Alex being only two and half would take the brunt of Kendall's anger. Angel walked to her moms' new home hoping to discuss the behavior of the new family members. Angel asked Lil to have a seat so they could talk about what was going on.

"Mom you have to open your eyes and see that these girls aren't normal, why put yourself in a situation that is completely out of your control. I know that your are in love but do you really want to spend many more years in such a mad household, these kids are crazy!" Angel said.

161

Before she could continue speaking, there was yelling going on outside. Ainsley wanted to walk to the store and Jeremy told her not right now, Ainsley started to throw one of her fits and as a result Ainsley hit Kendall across the back with a branch. Lil took it upon herself to ground Ainsley to her room. Angel noticed the evil in Kendall's eyes. Alex sat on Angels lap and held his ears while Ainsley screamed curses at their mom. Kendall then screamed out of control at Lil and begged for her to let Ainsley out so she wouldn't be mad any more. The yelling went on for thirty agonizing minutes and finally it just stopped and Alex wanted down from Angels lap to go and play. He walked toward the heavy front door and opened it acting as though he was going out.

"Alex stay in here no one is out there to watch you" Angel said in a stern voice.

Angel looked down the hall to make sure he was listening. But as always he tried to push her buttons leaving just his little hand in the door to keep it opened. Kendall slowly walked towards the door; she looked back at Angel with her lips curled up. She looked like a mad dog ready to attack. Angel watched to make sure she wasn't doing anything and as she watched, Kendall grabbed Alex's arm hard holding him in the door way, as Angel rushed towards him Kendall opened and then shut the door on his little fingers closing the door all the way. He let out the loudest scream looking at Angel in agony as she opened the door to let his hand free. Angel thanked God for Jeremy just two days before putting putty around the door frame to keep the cold air out; if it wasn't for the putty then the door could have taken his fingers. Angel rushed him to the kitchen and put ice on his fingers that had already turned blue.

Kendall just stood there with a grin on her face and in every ounce of her being Angel prayed to God to let her have patience and not hurt Kendall the way she wanted to. She kept reminding herself that Kendall was only seven. Just as Lil walked through the door and rushed towards Alex the grin on Kendall's face had turned into a frown and she began to scream over and over that she tried to pull him away from the door and no one but Angel and Alex knew the truth. Angel explained to her mom what really happened, but her mom turned a deaf ear and blamed Angel for accusing Kendall because she thought Angel was jealous and wanted her mom all to herself again and didn't want her to be happy.

Months went by of Angel telling her mom over and over about Kendall's behavior, but she never believed her. Blaming all of Alex's' bruises and cuts on his clumsiness. He then began to act out of control towards everyone around him. How could Angel blame him when their mom looked the other way again? Angel began to watch Alex every chance she got to keep him away from his house of torture.

Angel finally had to get away from everything and she planned a vacation to go visit her Dad, she took Alex and Diamond with her. Dwayne fought with Angel to stay claiming that he couldn't get time off from work. Angel found out a couple of days before leaving from Jeremy that while Dwayne was helping him on the garbage root, he had met a girl at the diner they ate at. Angel called and asked Dwayne about this woman and like always he denied even talking to her and vowed that nothing ever would make him cheat on her again. So Dwayne told Angel to go on her trip that way they had some alone time and he could make some more money while she was gone.

Dwayne began to do tattoos on people a couple of weeks before Angel left and he made Angel a promise that no women would be in the house while she was gone. Angel helped him make up the back room into a tattoo parlor that way he could really look professional. When it was time to leave Dwayne did everything but push Angel down the stairs getting her to hurry and leave. She gave him a kiss good bye and told him that when she returned things would be better.

Three days later she called him and he sounded great, she couldn't believe she had never missed him as much as she did right then. Angel missed his occasional hug and kiss. He seemed happy to hear from her and sounded as though he missed her also. Later that very night Angel called her mom and she was furious about something.

"Angel you need to come home now, for the past three nights Dwayne has had party after party. There also has been a girl over there day and night the same one from the diner". Lil yelled into the receiver.

"Mom don't tell him that you talked to me I will try to come home early and catch him cheating on me again" Angel said. The beginning of the following week she was on the road going back home. She was scared to confront him but she had to hear or see the truth for herself.

She tipped toed up the stairs in hopes of catching him before he had time to lure the girl out their bedroom window onto the roof. There he sat in the living room chair alone drawing a stencil for tattooing. Shirtless and with not a shame in the world while showing a necklace of hickies around his neck. Angel exploded and stomped out with Diamond, she brought her over to Lils so she wouldn't have to witness the anger and fighting with her dad for his stupidity. As Angel walked back home she thought of all the excuses he may use, but never could she have imagined the bullshit he had to say.

"Honey why in the hell did you come home early? I talked to you a couple of nights ago and you didn't mention coming home early. You are one sneaky bitch you planned on only staying for a week and came home trying to catch me doing something wrong. Then you have the nerve to walk in and give me attitude when you're the one lying about everything" he yelled. Angel couldn't believe her ears he was cheating yet putting the blame on her for doing something wrong. He would always manipulate her with his mind games blaming her before she could blame him this time she wasn't letting him do that she wanted to stick to her guns and leave him.

"Don't you dare pull this shit on me I already saw the hickies around your neck, was it that slut from the diner the one you have been flirting with every weekend on the garbage root. If it was then please leave me she looks more like your type, greasy hair, tattoos like a mans and not one ounce of class in her whole body" Angel yelled back. Still almost backing down with the tears streaming down her face.

"Angel these aren't hickies on my neck, there you go again bitching about something you don't know shit about. I was in a fight and he kicked me in the neck and it caused it to bruise. I would never cheat on you we were going to try and work this out. Why in the hell would I go and fuck it up. Brook is so fucking ugly she looks like a man, if I were to cheat on you which I'm not I would have better taste than that. You can ask anyone you are all I talk about" he began to cry. Then he began to name people that had seen this so called fight he had been in.

"We are done Dwayne; I don't believe you not even for a minute and please a bruise one that wraps around your neck. You have till tomorrow to get your stuff out and leave" she yelled pointing to his things everywhere.

Angel went to his tattoo room and began to pack his things. She noticed a stencil of a spider's web and on the bottom of it was Brooks's name.

"Dwayne was Brook here while I was gone" Angel asked.

"No there wasn't anyone here and I have never even talked to her before" he answered.

"Then what is this stencil doing here with her name on it and from the look of it, you have already used it. Oh don't tell me there is another Brook living in Lincoln maybe a guy with that name" she yelled waving the stencil around like a mad woman.

"That was a friend of hers and it's not used I spilled water near it and some got on it. Stop going through my shit if you want me out I will pack my things up. I'm going to get our daughter and you can tell her that her slut mother is kicking me out. Then explain to her why she won't ever see me again" he said walking out the door.

Angel pictured her little face covered with tears the same way Angels must have been when her mom left her Dad. Angel couldn't do it to her; she couldn't let her daughter look at her the same way she looked at her mom.

"Please stop this Dwayne just tell me the truth then we can talk this out I will ask Mom to keep Diamond for the weekend so we can work at this and talk about it all" Angel begged.

"OK but I already told you the truth I don't even know Brook. I saw her a few times at the diner and she sent a friend to the house for a Tat, Jeremy must have told her that I do tattoos. She never came over herself you can ask anyone" he said.

He was so convincing that Angel wanted to believe him, but she couldn't his story began to get longer and longer. Angel knew that he had cheated and would never admit to it, but she had to try for Diamonds sake. That night when they were suppose to talk Dwayne had invited a bunch of friends over to tattoo, he claimed not even telling Angel that Lil would watch Diamond so that they could talk. Angel begged him over and over again, that he needed to ask his friends to leave so they could work things out. He just bashed mean remarks at her in front of his friends, telling them how crazy she was always acting like a warden. She waited for two more hours and finally walked in again and reminded him of why Lil was watching Diamond.

"Cole she thinks that these are hickies around my neck. Didn't we get into a fight and you kicked me in the neck" Dwayne said gesturing to Cole to tell Angel what happened.

"Yeah we were assholes and drank way too much, and then we fought. I've been with him the whole time and there haven't been any girls over here while you've been gone" Cole said.

"Dwayne please I wouldn't believe him no more than I believe you" Angel said.

Finally everyone left and it was already two in the morning. Dwayne and Angel went to bed finally and Angel confessed to him that she thinks that they should break up for awhile.

"Ok but can we please make love one last time for old times' sake" he asked. They began to kiss and then the next thing she knew they were having the best sex that they ever had before. Afterwards they lay side by side without saying anything; they knew that it was all over. They were about to fall asleep in each other's arms when someone started banging on the door. Dwayne jumped up acting like it must have been a raid from the police. Angel asked him who might be knocking on the door at five in the morning.

"It must be an emergency, just stay here I will check it out" he said pushing her back onto the bed.

Angel lay in bed, but made sure that the door was opened enough for her to hear what was going on. At first all she could hear were whispers, fortunately the person he was talking to couldn't lower their voices and she heard all.

"I thought she was coming home next week, how are we going to see each other" the voice asked.

There was a moment of almost silence as Dwayne tried to explain.

"You don't understand my boyfriend found out about us and beat the fuck out of me. I have to go to the hospital; I think he broke a rib. Please come with me I don't care who knows about us now the worst is over" she cried and begged him to go with her.

He made his way back into the bedroom, without a word he began to put his clothes on.

"So do you want me to leave and come back in a week, then you can continue this so called affair that you didn't have" Angel said sarcastically.

"Don't even start its just Cole's girlfriend and he blew up when he found out that she got a tattoo. Remember you were here when she got it two weeks ago. I'm going with her to the hospital to make sure everything is alright. I'll be back in about an hour or so. I love you and I want this to work out, why would I go with a girl and fuck this all up after we just made love" he said.

"I know that isn't Cole's girlfriend and I've heard a lot more than you think. If you leave with her you can stay with her and don't bother coming back" Angel answered.

Then without another comment he was out the door. All night she thought of different reasons why she should stay and there wasn't any. He returned the following day at one in the afternoon. When he came into the house to change he had fingernail marks going down his back. His story was worst than the other one. They were walking up the hill Cole's girlfriend and himself and they saw Cole coming. Dwayne walked faster but Cole was mad and ran, then jumped on his back making the scratch marks.

That was his last story, Angel went into their bedroom and like a crazy woman she began to pack his things. She threw what ever she could get her hands on out the second story window onto the lawn. She noticed that this man had made her act crazy, unlike herself, throwing things, cursing, screaming.

"Come down here Sweetie" she heard a voice yell up to her, it was Dwaynes' mother.

"Everyone lies to their partners once in awhile. If you tell the truth all the time then no one would be happy. You need to toughen up and make this marriage work" she said.

He stayed at his mother's house for a few weeks and then he had the nerve to bring Brooke with him to get the rest of his things. Angel knew the truth but for reasons unknown she had to hear it from them. She finally had them both standing in front of her. Angel wanted to hurt Brooke and hurt Dwayne at the same time; they made Angel out to be the joke of the neighborhood. Just a stupid housewife who had no clue of what her own husband was doing with another woman. Dwayne finally admitted that they kissed, and then he stopped her. Angel could see in her eyes that there was more. She stood there looking like a deer caught in front of headlights. He began to cry and as she looked over she noticed Brooke rolling her eyes to his story. Angel couldn't believe a word he had said.

They all went their separate ways, and that night Angel began to feel sick. The nerves had gotten the best of her; she was throwing up and became really weak. The following day she began to spot some blood after going to the bathroom. She knew she had already had her period a few weeks ago and wasn't due to start until the following week. That day the pain began to increase she was in a fetal position unable to hardly move. Lil brought her to the doctor, convincing her that it was nothing, probably a nervous breakdown, it will go away.

"Angel it looks as though you are having a miscarriage, we will do all that we can to stop it" the Doctor said.

"What, I'm pregnant, but we haven't even been trying. Damn it, it was the night before I kicked him out" she explained it as though the Dr. would have some answers to what she should do.

Angel was indeed pregnant again. She wanted to be happy but she had no clue what Dwayne would say about it.

Little Dave

Age 20

Angel felt as though the right thing for the baby would be to wait before telling Dwayne, because of the stress Dwayne had put her through with the other pregnancies. A month went by and while she stayed strong and stayed away from him, he came to her. He had hurt himself falling off a roof, so he begged to stay with Angel and asked if she would please take care of him. The doctors told him to stay in bed for at least one month.

"Dwayne I should tell you something, I'm pregnant again" Angel said while handing him a tray with soup and milk on it.

"Well whose baby is it" he asked.

"I'm a couple of months along and the baby belongs to you. I got pregnant the last time we had sex, you know the night you left with Brook. I haven't been with anyone else just you" Angel cried.

"Ok you don't have to be a bitch about it. Can we work on things and stay together if not for ourselves for the children?" he asked hugging her like he just heard the best news ever.

"Yes let's at least try to stay together. No more cheating, lying or neglecting one another" Angel said hugging him back.

Two months later Angel went for her first ultrasound and tried to prepare herself for more bad news. It seemed as if it were a bad dream, she was in the same waiting room with the gray colored walls and pictures of mothers and babies all around looking back at her. The nurse came out and told Angel that it would be a few more minutes the doctor was running behind. Angel walked towards the rest room and knowing that she needed a full bladder for the ultrasound she just needed to be alone. She sat on the toilet and prayed to God.

"God I know that I have been asking you for a lot lately but things are going so well between Dwayne and me, I want it to last. But I have to wonder if they are going so good because I am pregnant and what would happen to our family if I wasn't? Please Lord let this baby live and be healthy, give me one more chance and I will make you proud".

"Well there is your baby, oh wait a minute; it looks as though there is another baby hiding behind that one" the Dr. said.

Angel listened as they let her hear her babies' heartbeats. They could hear two heart beats one was faint, but the Dr. said that was normal of twins. Angel couldn't believe it, they looked so healthy and moving so fast. Angel still watched the monitor waiting to hear bad news like before. Angel was relieved when the Dr. told her to leave and take care of herself and their babies. They went home and told everyone about the twins. Then like always they went shopping, for some reason shopping made Angel see the reality that she was indeed going to have their babies.

Angel began to pray each night and the following Sunday she began to go to church. Wondering if her neglect towards God in the past had caused this punishment and that's why he took her other babies away. Soon after she started to go to church she begged Dwayne to go with her and pray for their babies. He never did, she never understood why he was so against going to church seeing as he was raised Catholic and even went to a Catholic School. He made up for not going to Church when he sat and prayed with her at night. He was there for Diamond and played with her and smiled at her every move. They finally became a family.

Angel counted the days during her pregnancy, another day would go by and she would thank the Lord. Angel tried not to eat too much that way Dwayne would still want her, she knew how he hated fat girls and was turned off when she was pregnant with Diamond. Though the weight seemed to keep on, Angel knew it was because she had two babies inside her not just one. Some days were better than others with Dwayne, there were times that he would look at other women and comment on how skinny they were and ask her if she remembers how she looked when they first started dating.

Their happy family only lasted months then he began to flirt with other women right in front of Angel again and started having teenage girls over to admire him. Angel tried not to fuss over it too much, because she knew if she mentioned it he would always take the comment way too far and start a huge fight.

Angel became sick again with stress and she knew it was from keeping her anger and sorrow inside. Angel started to vent her problems to her mother and she would listen to her while she cried and complained about her own life.

"Mom I want to leave but I can't let Diamond be without a father the same way I was left without a father" Angel cried.

"Angel just stay and wait and see if things change after the babies, if things don't change you will have to leave and be happy without him" she said over and over again.

Lil would talk to Dwayne all the time always hoping that if someone else said how he was hurting Angel maybe he would listen. After these talks he would start to brainwash Lil into thinking that it was something that Angel had done wrong. No matter what Dwayne had to say, Lil would back her daughter and this made him furious.

After one of their usual fights Angel began to feel a familiar pressure and pain in her stomach. She ran to the bathroom and noticed that she began to spot as she collapsed to the floor and curled into a fetal position yelling for help. Dwayne ran towards the bathroom and began his own prayer to the Lord begging him to please let the babies be alright. The cry from Angel was all too familiar. As Angel looked at Dwayne while he walked her down the stairs to rush her to the hospital she couldn't help but blame him once again. He had no clue of the pain he brought her when they fought.

"I am having a miscarriage and I'm pregnant with twins please stop it" she cried out to the first person she saw.

Moments later Angel lay on a bed with her legs up in stirrups waiting to hear the fate of her babies again.

"Angel I believe that you were right you are having another miscarriage. Let's try to calm you down then we will do another ultrasound to check because I do hear a heartbeat and it's strong" the Dr. said.

They looked with question as they all saw a healthy baby moving and they looked closer to try and see the other baby. Finally they saw what looked like a baby but not moving at all and so much smaller than the baby in front. The most the doctor could do for Angel is to tell her to take it extremely easy and wait it out to see whether she has a miscarriage or not.

The following days she still bled and then the movement stopped all together. She told the family the news that she had a miscarriage and this seemed to give Dwayne the fuel he needed. He felt there was no need to hold back the fighting, flirting or neglect since there were no babies any more. She was scheduled to see the doctor a few days later; he said that if she was to miscarry he wanted to see her afterwards to make sure that she was ok. Angel felt in her heart that there were no babies.

Her next appointment she went by herself, it hurt to see the waiting room filled with happy expecting women. It was like watching TV, Angel wasn't really there, everyone else was so happy. It seemed routine to her now, going to the doctor to hear more bad news. When the doctor walked her into the room he looked at her with sorrow for her loss.

"Please, before anything let's get a urine test to make sure there's no infection" he said handing her a cup.

"Still spotting I noticed" he said.

"There's a little bit of bleeding still" Angel answered.

As he did the test by putting a piece of paper in the urine. He seemed shocked by the results of it.

"This can't be, if this is correct than you are still pregnant. We will take some blood and check it that way. Then I want you at the hospital for another ultrasound" he said.

Angel walked over to the hospital again and felt ridiculous asking for another ultrasound. Angel tried to call Dwayne, no answer at first, so then she tried again. He seemed very busy and said that he couldn't get to the hospital right then. Angel then went into the room that she had so many times before that showed her baby, dead! As the doctor applied the gel to her stomach he had a look on his face like a mad scientist that just found a miracle drug. Angel cried happy tears this time when she saw her baby moving all around on the screen.

Someone then knocked on the door and slightly opened it. Dwayne stood there with a sorry face. Angel was so happy to see him and all her madness went rushing out and she smiled.

"Honey we are still pregnant, come over here and see our baby boys" she said lovingly.

"Wait I don't see my other baby, where is the other baby the one that was hidden in back" Dwayne asked the doctor.

"Well I haven't seen this for quite some time, but it looks as though you miscarried one baby and the other one is still there. This baby looks healthy Angel. Your due date will be August 7. Please take it easy and I still want to see you next week just to do a follow up. If you begin to have more pain and if you start bleeding heavy call me right away" he said. The Nurse that was there with them printed out some ultrasounds of their baby. Angel went straight home and called the family to tell them that she was still pregnant. It seemed even silly to her that just one baby was still living but she thanked the Lord.

Angel talked more with her mom on how to help her marriage. Angel wanted to hear why her mother would leave her father if she knew that he was a good father. She wanted someone to tell her that everything would be ok if she stuck it out with Dwayne. "Angel your father couldn't stop cheating on me, I really wanted to stay with him so that you could be happy but he was never happy with me" she explained.

"Mom I think that is what makes me different from you I can fake being happy and I know that I need to stay with Dwayne in order to keep my children from being harmed. Dwayne may be an asshole to me but he is one hell of a good Dad" Angel explained.

There were more problems than her marriage she needed to tend to. The street that they lived on became really bad. At night she would lay there and listen to fights sometimes they got so loud that Diamond would wake up and cry because she was so tired. Every night the cops were there, the same way it was years ago when she lived on Homestead street. Sometimes in broad day light she would watch as a car drove up the hill and a teenager or two would jump out at it and smash the car with their bats or pipes for fun. She would often talk to Dwayne about moving because it just wasn't safe to raise the kids in this type of environment. He would puff up his chest and remark that they wouldn't dare come near them, they knew who he was and knew that he would "fuck them up!" if they tried anything. Most of the time he would act so tough in front of Angel, but when he came face to face with confrontation he backed down like a scared child being bullied.

Angel was able to get Diamond enrolled in a preschool they allowed three and four year olds to attend before entering kindergarten. Angel wanted her to get away from the neighborhood for a few hours during the day and interact with other toddlers her age. The first day of school Angel put Diamonds hair up in two ponytails and dressed her in a white sun dress that had blue pokka dots all over it. She looked so cute and when they walked in to her new school she acted as though she already owned the place. She somehow already knew that she needed to put her Barbie backpack in the cubby on the wall.

"Mommy this is my place, you can go now" she said, trying to push Angel towards the door.

"This must be Diamond. Can your mommy stay with us just today then she can see what you will be doing everyday here" Ms. Jean asked.

"Guess so, she can" Diamond answered shrugging her shoulders and winked at Angel, using the wink she just learned a week ago from Dwayne.

Angel could tell by watching her, she will be a leader, someone all the children will look up to. As the other children entered the room, it was Diamond at 31/2 who showed them around. The teachers seemed to adore her. Angel cried the next day when she had to fasten her seat belt on the bus and send her to school alone.

"Ok mommy, go" she said wiping away her mommies tears with her tiny hand. She waved goodbye as the bus drove off.

Angel watched and realized that this would be the first time someone other than Lil and Dwayne watched her. Angel couldn't help but worry thinking "what ifs" like how about if they let a man in and he sneaks her somewhere to hurt her, or maybe what if another father volunteers his time just to be able to touch her baby girl. Angel jumped in her car and raced down the street in order to watch the bus to make sure they didn't pick up any men with their children. While she was driving something crossed her mind how crazy it was but she didn't stop. She sat near the bushes like some sort of stalker watching in the windows at her baby girl. She sat there for three hours and then went home just to meet the bus and get Diamond back into her arms.

By time August came Angel only gained 14 pounds but she felt huge. She gave into her marriage and realized that it was what it was. Dwayne didn't want her sexually anymore than she wanted him but they have a family to raise and that is what she decided to do. They decorated the nursery three days before her due date to assure that she wouldn't give it any bad luck. The room was Mickey and Goofy; classic Disney.

On August 7th, she began to have contractions and waited till they were 5 minutes apart just like the doctor told her to. They went to the hospital and she was already 5 centimeters dilated. She was in labor for only 11 hours then at 9:05 pm their son little Dave was born, weighing 7 pounds and 5 ounces and 191/2 inches long. He was gorgeous, the biggest brown eyes anyone ever saw. Real dark hair and healthy. Dwayne seemed so proud, he had his boy.

They got what they wanted, they now were complete they have a boy and a girl in perfect health. As for Angel the doctor said that with all her complications it was in her best interest to stop at two. If she were to have another baby there was no guarantee that neither she nor the baby would make it past delivery. As she laid there with her baby boy attached to her breast sucking the weight out of her, slowly drifting off to sleep, she noticed Summer at the age of twelve she sat in the corner stiff, frightened. As she walked towards Angel she let her know that after watching something so gross happen to her she would never have any children.

Little Dave was her miracle baby boy; he is a survivor like her. He lost someone he loved, his twin brother and he still had the strength to come out a fighter and face this world. She knew by the look in his eyes he will grow to be a person who fights for life and gives a chance to people who need encouragement. The same strength he found in himself.

After going home Dwayne again seemed like a changed man, time would tell how long it would last. They decided that after hearing guns going off outside their building that it was time to start looking for a new home to raise their wonderful children.

The Accident

Angel went over to her moms one day to do some laundry. As she walked into her house she noticed that no one was there but she knew her mom wouldn't mind her using her washer. As she walked down the stairs she felt this strange feeling in her stomach that something was wrong. When she walked back upstairs the phone rang. An unfamiliar voice asked if she had seen Lillian.

"No but that is my mother can I take a message" she asked.

"Yes this is Robbie and I think that I just saw your mother in a car accident and wanted to make sure it wasn't her" he said.

"Oh my God" she yelled dropping the phone on the floor and picked up Diamond and Dave then ran to the car.

Angel got into her car and found herself driving behind an ambulance. It was as though someone else was driving her to the hospital where she would find her mother. She waited and watched while the men got out of the ambulance and took the bed out of the back which held someone that looked nothing like her mother. She ran into the hospital and asked someone if there was a woman who had just been in a car accident rushed there. As she was told to go to the emergency room and ask, she felt a hand touch her back. She turned around to find her little brother Alex frighten and scared and asking for his mom. She bent down to hug him and a police officer asked her to follow him into the other room.

"Your mother was in a very bad car accident she's in with the doctors right now. I will go and let them know that you are here and you would like them to tell you how she's doing as soon as possible" he said.

All they could do was wait, as she sat there the word got out about Lil and soon the waiting room was full of friends and relatives, all waiting to see how she was doing. Finally after a few hours the doctor came out and stood in front of them as though he had prepared a speech to tell everyone.

"Your mother has a few things wrong with her some minor and some not so minor. Her leg is broken very badly. But the first thing that we have to worry about is that she has some internal bleeding. We will need to rush her to another hospital where there are more surgeons who specialize in this. You can go see her before she leaves but please be quick" he said.

Angel walked in a room that had 6 or 7 doctors standing around the same woman who looked nothing like her mother. This woman that she looked at was swollen and her flesh was white. Angel wouldn't have believed that this woman was her mother if the doctors didn't just tell her. As she stood at the head of the bed she fell into a daze and envisioned Leon standing over her mom's bed smiling while her life lay in the Doctors hands. The same way her life had been put into his hands so many times. The doctor led Angel out of the room and she asked

"Will she live?"

"I have to tell you with all of the problems she's having you might want to get your pastor or priest in there to pray for her" he answered.

Angel knew by looking at her that she might not make it. She called the pastor and told him what had happened, also that she would like him to pray for her. It only took him a few minutes before he was there beside her and praying that she would make it and that the Lord would allow her to fight for her life. Then she was rushed to Dartmouth Hitchcock Medical Center Hospital and Angel drove there in what seemed to be endless hours.

She waited in that unconformable waiting room watching as people came and went until 1:30 am. Finally someone came out to inform her that her mother was very lucky to still be alive. The surgery was a success, but there was some sacrifice. She may never be able to walk again, her pelvic bone was fractured very badly and her leg was broken and needed immediate surgery.

Dwayne stayed by Angel's side the whole time and as he was in there more people showed up waiting to make sure that the surgery went well. The police officer that Angel spoke to was hesitant in telling her that a 16 year old had borrowed her fathers' new truck and was speeding as her mother tried to take a turn. The girl didn't have time to slow down and crashed into the drivers' side of her mothers' car.

Alex, for the first time Angel could remember stayed in his booster seat and because of that he only had a bruise on his leg.

Angel went in for one last time that day to see her mom; she was still in a daze from all the medicine they gave her. But she smiled and said thank god she was wearing clean underwear. She was such a clean person and that statement alone was proof that she hadn't lost her sense of humor.

Angel kept Alex and Summer with her. Their Mom had to stay in the hospital for two months but she made sure that they went to see her at least three times a week. The hospital was an hour and half away and all of them got car sick from driving. Alex would pitch a fit when he was in the car but Angel knew that it probably was because of the accident and he was still scared. Summer took it ok without her mom but she was used to being away from home anyway because she was a teenager now. Alex took it much harder; he was never away from their mom even over night at someone else's house.

Angel was ok knowing that every time she talked to her mom she said that she hasn't felt any pain do to the medication. Sometimes when she would see her she would take a moment outside to prepare herself because she looked so sore, her leg up in pins and her body was still swollen. At times Aunt Ann went with her that way she could pray for her sister asking God to answer their prayers that Lil would be able to walk and get out of the hospital soon. At times she wanted to go with Angel but she had her own problems at home. Her husband James; began to drink heavily and smoking more pot. He was always abusive emotionally towards Aunt Ann but recently became physically abusive as well. Angel never understood why she stayed with him, but she would tell Angel that the Lord wanted her there no matter what he put her through.

Lil became very tough in the hospital and refused to leave without walking on her own. She pushed herself everyday during physical therapy. All her efforts and determination showed the day she was released when she walked out of the hospital with only using a cane. Still to this day one leg is a couple of inches shorter than the other.

Alex was very happy to have their mom home and so was everyone else. Angel loved him so much but she still admits he was a handful. Summer was only 14 and acted as though she didn't care one way or another. Angel knew that she cared, just by the look in her eyes, every time she looked at her mom, she would tear up.

Things at Lil's house got worse as time went on. They found out that Ainsley had been molesting Kendall for quite some time. Angel always knew that something was going on but she couldn't put her finger on it. Lil and Jeremy sent her away to get some help, hoping that being away from Ainsley for awhile Kendall could get help also. After awhile she heard about some more molesting in the family, it was as though their family was cursed with this. At one time or another most of the girls and a few boys were molested by someone in the family. Angel took it as her job to open everyone's eyes to it and get the help they needed very early.

As for Dwayne and Angel, they became distant again while she was helping her mom. He put himself into his tattooing and blamed her for not wanting their marriage to work, she did but her family came before her happiness. She would stay up all night with little Dave and Diamond when they couldn't sleep, while Dwayne had a house full watching him tattoo. Every time she talked with him it was another fight. He would say things like "I'm doing this for us, to get us out of here, we need money" or "If you wouldn't be such a cunt and think you are better than everyone you would come and sit with us". She would remind him that her job is to take care of their children and if he was doing all of it for the money than she should see some bills being paid!

Her New Prison

AGES 21 - 24

They did eventually move to Cranberry Lane and they were happy because it was still in Lincoln. There were a lot of other kids in the complex that Diamond and Dave could play with. Angel was in hopes that this would be their final move, making this the right place to raise their children. The kids seemed very happy at the new place and seeing their smiles made it easier to hide her tears.

Efforts made to save her marriage became harder every day. She would tell herself with every new coat of paint that their marriage could be saved; If only that was the case? She wanted to start over, start from the beginning when they were still friends and loved each other and believed that their love was strong enough to overcome anything.

During some of their fights Dwayne would tell her that she couldn't leave him, reminding her of how he stood by her during the whole Leon thing. Every fight became routine, he would yell, scream and call her names, throwing things or slamming doors. Then if she didn't respond to him the way he wanted her to he would then drag the kids into it. Telling them how their mother was nothing but a slut and how she doesn't love him anymore and wants him to leave and never come back.

To make things worse he would call her mother and have her on the phone for hours as he whined about what a bad person her daughter was and how he has tried his very best, to make things work! No one really saw the Dwayne that she saw and knew or the father that the kids knew. Most of their friends admired their relationship, the one where he treated her so well and she did everything for him, then later after everyone left he would turn into the man she hated.

The next three years went the same way, they would fight and she would concede and again try to work their marriage out. There were times that he would go months without touching her at all and still hating him begging for something, anything to make sure she was still alive! They split up a few times, she then would find someone who treated her the way she should be and wanted to be treated. Dwayne then would threaten them, by moving back into her house. Sometimes she would wait for fights to begin and end; because that was the only time she would receive flowers, love notes and a whole lot of "I'm sorry!"

He put a lot of his time into his tattooing and partying. She and the kids would stay in their bedrooms hoping that at some point the noise would stop. Sometimes he would play mind games so well he had her believing that she might very well be to blame for their fights.

One day on one of her regular walks past Sandy beach she stopped suddenly almost crumbling to the ground, her chest hurt so badly and the pain was indescribable. She realized she was afraid to go home and see him, she wanted the fun that she and the kids had at the beach to continue, and she didn't want Dwayne to ruin it. She felt trapped in the same way she had felt years ago with Leon. She sat for hours and let the kids play while she thought of why she was still with him, she knew that she truly hated him and walked on eggshells when ever he was around, praying that she wouldn't say the wrong thing and upset him, also hoping that her family wouldn't come over and upset him by being in their house or trying to keep the kids quite so he wouldn't get angry from their noise. She knew how mean he really was and she wanted it to end, she was done with him!

She knew she had to tell him how she felt, so finally she got up the courage to talk to him. She sent the kids over to her mother's house. She sat him down and told him that she wanted a divorce, he begged and promised to change and this is what went on for the following two years. He would try for a few weeks and it was like letting a wild animal loose ready to pounce on the first person he saw. Then she would tell herself to try and stay for the kids, and then when they are old enough she would leave!!

Angel kept telling herself that he would change, but there was someone changing and it was her. She became mean and cold to everyone. She began cheating on him just to feel wanted by someone. Angel knew inside she was still a nice person who would help anyone in need.

She began to work at a factory making very low wages, she hated going home; there were times she believed the kids would be better off with someone else who would be a better mother to them.

Sometimes it takes something very small to change your life and that is what happened. On this day, Dave who was four and in preschool and Diamond who was in second grade sat at the table and asked her to leave the room. Angel wondered what they were up to, she heard laughing and paper cutting. "Mommy, come in now we made something for you" Diamond yelled.

Angel walked in and they handed her a paper with their hands traced on it, and underneath in Diamonds hand writing the caption read "You the best mom ever" and under that was a scribble that Dave said he wrote down, "mommy I love you big". This was the sign she needed to regain her life and be that mom she knew she and as her kids knew she was the best and only mother for them.

The following day she went to sign up for her GED and worked extra hard at the library after work so Dwayne wouldn't know and tease her about it. She knew nothing past the eighth grade, and in order to gain a better life, she would have to work extra hard to pass. There were times she looked at the borrowed GED book from the library and cried wondering how she would ever pass, it seemed like a different language to her.

It was finally the day of the test and as she opened the high school doors she ran straight to the bathroom and threw up. She sat in a hard leather chair in a cubical with the test in front of her. Angel had to pass a test that was the equivalent of a high school education. In just two hours she was finished, she felt like she rightly answered a lot of the questions and may have passed. They said they would send the test scores in the mail: she would just have to wait.

That night she called her mom and told her that she had taken the test, her mom was so proud of her and Dwayne claimed to be proud also. The next morning she knew what she was going to do if she passed the GED. Someday she would own her own business and do what she loved to do.

Angel told Dwayne her plan that day and didn't realize how crazy it sounded until he told her that she could never do it all. Getting her GED was one thing but College didn't seem probable. As she left to check for the mail box for her scores she thought what if Dwayne was right! Maybe she was being crazy, maybe her fate was working in the factory like the rest of the family. Then she had the envelope in her hand afraid to open it. She went inside and started to cry even before she saw the score there it was, she had failed, and she broke down. She read her scores and they were broken down to every subject, she had only failed by seven points.

Angel knew that just seven points wasn't going to hold her back. She couldn't listen to Dwayne anymore, she had to be strong. She would get that GED and become someone that her kids could be proud of. She wanted them to be able to tell people that their mother was an important person. She signed up for night classes to get help on the subjects she needed work on. She barely saw the kids anymore and Dwayne would make her feel very guilty about that but she knew it wouldn't be long before they were all away from him.

A few months later she was standing in a room full of people and thanking the teacher who helped her pass her GED. She looked over to see Diamond and Dave's beautiful smiles while they clapped as she was handed her certificate of completion. She called everyone that night and her Dad said he was so proud of her. This was the first time he had really said it, she knew that she would make everyone proud especially when she finished college.

As she waited to talk to someone about financial aide and her courses she looked at the booklets, she noticed younger people than herself walk in and out of the office. This made her feel foolish; she was just now going to college after being married and having two children. She enrolled for business courses and in her head she could hear Leon and Dwayne laughing at her, that didn't stop her because now she was a college student! Some of the work was easy but most of it was a challenging. She loved the feeling she had knowing that someday she would be independent. She was wrong about all the young people; there were a lot of people her age taking these classes. She made many new friends that helped her and she helped them. She started to hang out at one of her new friend's house and they would work on their homework together, at times she would bring the kid's down with her, that way they could get away from Dwayne as well.

Most of the time Dwayne would accuse her of cheating on him, yet she felt as though when she left the house that her life was her own. In one sense she was the house wife, the sad, mean and withdrawn Angel. The other a strong, confident, smart, beautiful and happy woman. She became so mad at being falsely accused that she began to tell Dwayne that if he didn't pay more attention to her then she would find someone else to satisfy her.

She went to him and told him that she wanted it all to end. She couldn't stand him anymore; she was too old to put up with all of the shit he gave her on a daily basis. She couldn't put up with him anymore. It came to the point that she didn't even want him to touch her. She hated him, she hated her best friend! She wanted a divorce, but he wouldn't leave. He wanted her to move out, she thought about it and decided if he wouldn't leave, then she would. She moved over to her mother's house. This decision finally gave her the push she needed to really talk to her mom. Angel let everything out she told her how he really treated her. Angel did try to talk to Dwayne and tell him that they would be better off apart as friends. He blamed her for everything, her mother had heard about her affairs and people whom she hadn't slept with.

A couple of weeks went by and she knew it shouldn't be her moving out, she needed to get him out so she could raise her children in their home. He started one of his biggest fits, she called the police and even when they showed up Dwayne was at his worse.

As she turned around she noticed Diamond there in the corner holding Dave's ears. Everything that Leon did to her mother in front of them all come back to her. She knew right then she never wanted Dwayne again. That night the officers pulled Dwayne out of the house and both of the kids blamed Angel. They also hated those police officers for taking their Daddy away.

Dwayne's mother called her a few nights later to tell her that Lance (Dwayne's brother) found him in the woods. He threatened to kill himself if she didn't go back to him. She told all of them including Dwayne that she would be more than willing to help him but she was not taking him back.

Her life became like a tragic love story, one that went terribly wrong and crazy.

Dwayne began to play dirty; he did things that she never even imaged him stooping so low. He found her journal the one she had written in since she was eleven. He sold copies for a dollar to all the people Angel had recorded in her private journal. When she heard about this of course Angel was mad as hell and wanted revenge, but first she wanted a divorce before she did anything else.

She decided that he wouldn't bring her down no matter what tricks he pulled. She stayed in college and took all the classes that they would allow her to take. Her grades were higher because she had to stop thinking about Dwayne she put all her thoughts into her homework. Her grades were at a 3.9 in all her classes. She worked hard to make the money to feed her kids; because of course Dwayne wouldn't help her in any way. He thought that if he made it really hard on her she would go running back to him; at least, that is what he told some of his friends.

The courts said that it would take up to four months before their case could be heard. Dwayne seemed very busy finding his own life without

Angel, but kept her under his thumb at the same time with roses, gifts and nightly trips to her home made her begin to love him again. Meanwhile on the other side of town he had a young woman that thought she was the only one in his heart. When Angel found out all the hurt, pain and anger hit her all at once. Angel tried not to act jealous, but she was, she was jealous that this new woman was probably getting the Dwayne who she loved in the beginning. The sweet one that would do anything for anybody including her. Angel finally saw this new one from a distance with Dwayne and when she saw them together she knew that this woman wasn't getting the Dwayne who neglected to touch his wife for months, the one who would rather smoke pot with his friends than spend time with his own children.

Angel wondered did they look alike, was she thin like he wanted her to be, did she worship the ground he walked on the way Angel once did. Angel made every excuse to go see him. Angel found out where he was living and as she walked up the stairs to their apartment, she could smell pot lingering at the bottom of the stairs. She knocked on the door and could hear people scrambling inside as if to hide something. Dwayne finally came to the door and opened it just enough for him to slide through and push her away.

"Well why can't I come in, I want to meet her. Does she know that just last week you were at my house begging me to sleep with you and take you back?" she asked him.

"No she doesn't, and she doesn't have to, I'm with her and as soon as you take me back I will leave her. She is just a toy for me, she means nothing" he replied.

He opened the door all the way and a cloud of smoke rushed out. Angel finally saw her and jealousy took over the confidence that she once had. She was so young, so skinny, dark skin and long beautiful brown hair. Angel found out later that she was not quite seventeen yet, and she was mad at Dwayne because he was 28. Angel thought hard because she knew that she had seen this girl somewhere before, she remembered her being at the house weeks before Angel and Dwayne split up and in the basement smoking and partying with Dwayne. Angel wondered where her parents were and why would they let their daughter hang out and live with such an older man.

Angel made an agreement with the kids that Dwayne would have them over his house every other weekend and he wouldn't smoke pot and party around them. Angel didn't agree to this so easily but the courts said that he could get her for kidnapping if he wasn't aloud to see his own children. After two weekends he was still smoking, he didn't seem to care if he lost his time with the kids; all that mattered to him was his new toy girlfriend.

Their divorce finally became legal and on the outside they both seemed happy about it. Dwayne finally admitted that he was upset a little and would like to have his family back someday. They had newly divorced couples fights, mostly over the fact that this new woman "Girl" (Jasmine was her name) would smoke pot with the kids around, and Angel was totally against this. Angel didn't care who Dwayne was with as long as they treated the kids' great and didn't do anything around them that would harm them.

One of their fights got totally out of hand and Dwayne said he wanted a paternity test done on Diamond. He already knew deep inside that she wasn't his but he wanted to put Angel through as much pain as he could. She told him no at first because all that mattered was that he was her daddy and his name was the one on the birth certificate. He threatened if she didn't get one done then he would tell Diamond who her real father was. Diamond was only eight and when they first had her they agreed they would wait until she was much older to tell her about Leon. Dwayne was becoming this dirty man who would do anything to piss off Angel and hurt her, even at the expense of his children. He knew the only way to really hurt her was through them. He began to black mail her any way he could think of. She finally agreed to the test because she would rather tell Diamond then to have him do it.

Angel knew before these tests where done she would have to talk with the only other person who really knew who Diamonds biological father was and it was about time he came clean. It was time for Angel to go and talk to Leon but first she would have to talk with his mother who was the only person he kept in contact with.

"Hello Grammy Kramer please don't hang up this is Angel. I need to talk to you about Leon and Diamond" Angel said holding the phone so tight that her fingers went numb.

"Angel I'm not sure why you dare to call my house, but Leon has wanted to talk to you and apologize for all that he has done. Leon has had your name on the visitors list for awhile now"

"Grammy I am letting you know that Dwayne wants a test done to see if Diamond is his and we both know that she belongs to Leon. Please give Leon this number and tell him to call me" she said and hung up the phone.

The very next day Leon called and they scheduled a time for Angel to go and see him. Two weeks later Angel was sitting outside the prison trying to figure out what to say to this man that ruined her life. She had on her most mature outfit making sure to show as little skin as possible, but when she looked in the mirror before she left she could swear she looked like she was 16 again and going to a distant relative's funeral. Her hair was in a tight bun that gave her a headache after only an hour. She didn't put any makeup on in fear of that she might cry and it would run. She walked towards the building looking down the whole time noticing the pavement had just been redone and still a bit sticky. As she came closer she noticed fresh flowers on either side of the walk way. She only wondered why they would put fresh flowers outside of this awful looking building that is holding these criminals in it if they never see them.

She opened the door to dead air. She put her name on the visitors list and waited for them to call her. As she walked through the security she felt like a criminal the officers looking at her wondering what she might have on person. An officer walked her to a table that was far from the door leading outside. She asked him to please put her closer to the door just in case she has a hard time and needs to leave.

"Sweetie if you are so afraid to be here than just leave and maybe come back when you are more prepared" he said.

"I wish I could but I have no choice it's now or never. Thank you for giving me a different table and sorry for the inconvenience" she said politely.

"No problem just let me know if you need anything else. Don't worry there will be three officers in here the whole time" he replied assuredly. Angel knew deep inside that she wasn't afraid of what Leon would do to her because he had always been a coward and done everything in private. She was afraid of what she might do to him if she feels trapped.

Angel sat and looked all around and saw other prisoners who looked so young she wondered what they did that sent them to prison. She watched the door that all the other prisoners had come through to see their visitors and finally after what seemed like an hour Leon walked through the heavy grey door. Angel's hands began to shake and sweat, she could feel them become wet under her palms. As he got close she began to smell that same odor she smelled every time he got on top of her. He sat down across from her and smiled like he was visiting a long lost friend. Angel wanted to hit him she wanted to put her hands around his throat and strangle him. She wanted to feel his last breath on her face. She wanted him dead, for everything he put her through. Then finally she thought of why she was really here and wouldn't be here if it wasn't for Dwayne.

"Leon one of the times that you raped me when I just turned sixteen, I became pregnant and my ex husband wants a blood test done for our daughter" Angel said.

"Angel I will do anything to help you out, I'm sorry for everything that I have done to you in the past and I hope someday you can find it in your heart to forgive me" he answered.

Angel stayed there for almost two hours and told him everything she felt towards him, giving him little opportunity to respond, he sat there and listened. He offered to pay for everything and also agreed to pray that Diamond belonged to Dwayne. She wondered if the same Lord that ignored her many prayers when she was younger would listen to Leons.

In the following weeks she waited for his check in the mail, she called for an appointment at the hospital for the blood test. Dwayne agreed that he was always going to be Diamonds daddy but he just needed to know. The courts had already taken Leon's blood to check it compared to a sample of Diamonds. In the hospital room Dwayne held Diamond and he began to cry because he knew that in just weeks they would know her fate.

Weeks later an envelope was hand delivered by the mailman. She knew what it was but was afraid to open it. Angel went to her friend's house and sat with her, she agreed to open it for Angel and the look on her friends face told her she had information that Angel didn't want to hear.

"Angel I'm so sorry" she said and handed her the papers.

Angel read them and slumped to the floor; she woke up in her friend's arms. Angel read that Leon was in fact her daughter's real father. She ran all the way to Dwayne's and banged on the door to tell him the results.

"Here is the news that you couldn't wait to find out, now you can sit her down and tell her what you couldn't wait to that you aren't in fact her father" Angel yelled throwing him the papers as she turned running down the stairs.

Angel sat at the bottom of the stairs for what seemed like forever, she couldn't move, and then she heard Dwayne scream in pain. Angel walked home and knew that she would have to be the to tell Diamond the news because she didn't want Dwayne to tell her. Diamond sat on her moms lap as she told her and taking in her every word.

"Mommy I'm ok I know who my real daddy is. This just means that

I have a lot of other sisters and brothers and a bigger family" she said hugging Angel.

Angel wondered how she raised such an understanding little girl. She knew that she would have to tell Summer and Tony, that their niece was really their sister. She knew that Leon was to blame for the hell her family was going through, but she couldn't help but feel if Dwayne wasn't such an ass then none of this would have come up at all. She knew if he would have left it alone and be the daddy Diamond needed then he wouldn't have had hurt her at such a young age. He should have let Angel tell Diamond when she was old enough to understand a little better. Angel felt Diamond never had a real daddy, someone who thinks of their kids feelings before their own. A daddy who treats his children like, they are all that matters and would do anything to make them never feel pain or sorrow.

Angel finally told Summer and Tony, both of them were mad, hurt and pissed off. They were both old enough to realize how Diamond was conceived and if they didn't already hate their father enough now they wanted him dead. They both still couldn't love Diamond any more than they already did and till this day they are still Diamonds Auntie and Uncle.

Time went by and Diamond began to ask about Leon, what did he look like and what he sounded like.

"Honey Leon isn't a very nice man and I would rather not let you see him than for you to be disappointed"

"But Mommy why is he bad, why can't he be a good man"

"I'm sure honey that he was once a sweet boy. Then something bad happened to that little boy and made him make some very wrong choices"

Angel talked to a counselor about their situation and asked her what she should do about Diamond. She answered her bluntly and said that if she wants to meet her father then it was out of pure curiosity and she should let her meet him. But, if Angel never let her meet him and something should happen to him then she would most likely always blame her mom for not letting her know who he was. Angel couldn't live with herself if she were to blame for her not knowing him.

A year went by and Diamond still wanted to meet him and became angry at the fact that Angel wouldn't let it happen. Angel still can feel that pain in her stomach, how it felt when she saw her baby girl next to him. Diamond asked him all sorts of questions and what his family was like. He answered all her questions and they left it at that. She next wanted to meet Leon's mother and Angel thought that would be fine she never had anything against his mother. If anything she felt sorrow in her heart for her she couldn't imagine how she would feel if Dave had done the things Leon had done to a little girl. "Grammy" they all called her invited them into her home with open arms. She treated them both like her grandchildren.

Two and a half years went by and Angel's life was finally going uphill. Sometimes there were the occasional divots in the road, Dwayne was still begging for her to be with him, every romance she tried to have he ruined it all while being with Jasmine.

Angel received her degree and graduated with a 3.9. The school gave all the graduates tickets for their families to come to the graduation. Angel invited her Mom, Dad, Diamond, Dave, Summer and Alex. She had a couple of tickets left and decided that she wanted Dwayne to see what she had accomplished he accepted the ticket only if Jasmine could come. She believed that she owed some of this graduation to him if he hadn't been so cruel then she wouldn't have gone this far. Angel could remember hearing someone say what doesn't kill you will only make you stronger and the things that she went through in her life she believed in that.

The next few years Angel began to except Jasmine into her life, being where she would now be her children's step mother. Angel wanted someone for herself and for the children, but still every time she would find someone Dwayne would disagree about them. Angel didn't get to choose his new girlfriend but for some reason he made it very difficult for her to find someone. He would tell her that they weren't step father material, but she never brought them home around the children unless she dated them for more than six months then they could meet her family. There were only two men that she liked a lot but Dwayne chased both of them away.

She finally gave up and was single for another year. She was lonely and happy all at the same time. She knew that she was raising her children the way she wanted to. Angel did meet someone but she felt she had to keep her new romance a secret. She couldn't let the family; know that her new lover was a female. She wasn't ready for them to push someone else away. One day at school her friend introduced her to this beautiful woman named Chanel. This woman was perfect, smart, and beautiful and the first time Angel looked at her she knew that she was in trouble. Angel found every reason to meet up with her. They began to meet each other to do school work, then one night Chanel invited Angel to go out with her to the local club. When they met up downtown Angel couldn't believe how incredible Chanel looked she had only seen her in jeans and t-shirts for school.

They danced and what Angel thought was flirting all night. The club was closing and Angel didn't want the night to end. The kids were at her moms for the night so she invited Chanel back to hang out. As they walked back to Angels house Chanel stopped and turned Angel around.

"I have wanted to do this for so long" she kissed Angel.

Her sweet lips pulled Angel in and she could taste the sweetness rush beyond her lips and into her mouth. They stayed up all night laughing and kissing. When the sun began to raise them both woke up at the same time and Angel looked at this gorgeous woman beside her and felt like she finally found herself.

"Good Morning precious" Angel said as her hand began to pull Channels shirt up revealing this perfectly curved body.

They made love for hours and Angel knew this is where she belonged she knew she was meant to be with a woman not a man.

Chanel became Angel's best friend, she confided in her and Angel confided in Chanel. Angel became this other person one even stronger than before she tried not to fall in love but the harder she tried the deeper it got. As much as she concentrated on hiding her from her crazy family and only saw her every other weekend. Angel soon found out that Chanel also had to keep hidden when one day Angel finally met her mother and Chanel introduced her as her friend. Not girlfriend just friend. Angel fell in love with her over the next couple of years, she finally told her the way she felt and wanted them to come out to their families so that they could be happy and as one. Angel was crushed when Chanel then let her know that it could never happen she will never come out and that was that. Still unto this day she is Angel's true friend and still sees her every now and then. Over the years they remained best friends and nothing will ever change that. Chanel is still alone and she still talks about men when everyone else is around, but when they are alone Angel knows how she really feels.

Angel has begged her to stop pretending to be someone she really isn't. She has spent half of her life pretending to be straight, but Angel hopes that one day she will find someone she can love openly and not care what everyone else thinks.

The Rest Of Her Life

Her Heaven

She was happy but not fulfilled; she wanted to be a business woman. She went store to store determined to be a manager all her life someone always managed her she wasn't going too settle for less. Although she knew in reality she would have to start at the bottom. The stores continued to tell her that she was over qualified for the jobs they were offering, this made her happy to hear that, but she needed a job. She went to a very popular and large department store and when her interviewer looked her up and down she became nervous. She didn't want the job because of her looks that wasn't why she spent the last two and a half years at collage. Then she felt like a million dollars when he ask the question of why would she want to start at the bottom. Then he asked her where she saw herself in five years.

"I see myself at the highest level that you can achieve in only five years" she answered. She got the job as a cashier. She knew she would become more and was up for the challenge.

Only three weeks went by then she became a CSM- Customer Service Manager. She loved feeling in charge. She got to know all of her 22 cashiers, she had fun yet she knew that her job was to make the store run smooth. She realized after a year of working there and conversations between herself and the manager there would never be a woman manager. She decided that the best thing for her is to start a career and not just a job. She wanted to prove Leon wrong she knew that she could do the job that she always wanted to do and become a hairdresser. She went and signed up to become a cosmetologist at Empire Beauty School.

She still had to stay at work to have money to live on. She went to Dwayne and told him her plans of becoming a hairdresser. For some reason it meant a lot for her to have Dwayne proud of her, it meant even more to her to hear that he would support her every bit of the way. In all her transition from girl to woman, worker to manager, school to career she thought is was time to tell the kids that she was gay. She knew that now her business life was on the right path she still was so lonely and she also knew she wasn't going to settle down with a man. Diamond took it well and Dave was really upset. She let both of them know that just because she was gay it didn't mean that everyone needed to know. That was Diamonds biggest concern, that all her friends would find out and wouldn't like her anymore. She knew that it would be ok because even when she did date someone she never flaunted her relationships in front of the kids. She felt that she wasn't quit ready to tell the whole family but after telling the kids she felt that she was ready to start dating woman even if the kids never saw it. Without telling all her friends she still found it ok to be herself when they all went out dancing. She danced with woman and just let go of all the embarrassment that she had been holding on to for so many years.

At work the manager asked her to hire some new people for cashiering. One day two friends came in and asked for a job. As she interviewed the shy one she couldn't help but look at the other. She loved her job and the new hires worked out she was proud of the new people she hired she had a good sense in knowing who would work hard for her. She got along great with the new hire Meghan the one that she couldn't help looking at during the interview. The second thing she noticed about Meghan was she always wore this rainbow colored bracelet. Which apparently people in the gay world new that rainbow indicated a sense of gayness. She started listening to Meghan while she talked to other people in the break room. What struck Angel as odd was she was nothing like the women Angel usually went for and it struck her even more to realize how disappointed she was when she heard she had a boyfriend.

Time went by and she kept her secret about being gay from work and the rest of the family. She was certain some people assumed what they wanted but she didn't change her appearance or the way she was except she was smiling a lot more. She listened as people at work told gay jokes and she watched as Meghan rolled her eyes at them. She was still convinced that she was gay and all that talk about having a boyfriend was probably just a cover-up at work. Who knows, she did it for many years and no one had a clue that she was gay. She and Meghan worked together for a year and a half then Meghan went away for a few months. Angel tried to forget about Meghan but she couldn't get her out of her mind.

Things at home were at a standstill. Dwayne and Jasmine had a baby and he calls Angel "Auntie". The kids were finally getting along with Jasmine and Angel felt as though she would be single forever, unless she came out to the family, then, finally she would find a woman who would make her complete. She first told Summer and it went well she was happy for her but she admitted that she had always known she and Alex thought Angel might have been gay. Summer was 20 and Alex was 13. She wanted to keep it a secret from her mom and the rest of them a little longer. Different things would come up every time she felt brave enough to tell everyone. It would be another birthday or holiday or a family member was getting a divorce. She couldn't seem to find the right time to tell her mom.

It wasn't long as she had hoped after telling Summer when out of the blue after a fight Angel and Summer got into, when they were in the car driving Summer blurted out in front of Lil that Angel was gay. Summer was still raging towards people and if she was sad and angry everyone around her was sad and angry.

Lil pulled over after hearing the news and asked Angel if she was gay after Angel answered with the truth Lil cried and cried then she admitted that she had no clue what she was crying for, she didn't care if Angel was gay.

"I do think that you should tell the kids and stop hiding from everyone and let yourself be happy" Lil said. What she didn't know was the kids and her siblings already knew.

This amazed Angel that every time she told anyone about her being gay they all replied in the same manner they always worried about her because she always seemed to be sad. She was kinda mad because after all these years she thought that she was hiding the sadness.

One day as she sat at her computer and went online to find new hairstyles she saw Meghan's name pop up. Angel wrote her back to tell her hello and asked her how everything was going. She replied telling Angel that she would be home soon and come back to work full time. Angel just started typing and before she knew it she was flirting and Meghan was flirting back.

A couple of weeks went by and Meghan returned to work. Angel felt strange when she discovered that she had missed Meghan. Time went on and she flirted with Angel and asked her out a few times. Angel refused telling her that she was too young for Angel because she was in fact 9 years younger, Angel felt as though she had lived so much more than Meghan. She held back but felt herself becoming more and more attracted to her

Meghan had cut her hair real short into a fade and lost a lot of weight. Angel found Meghan hot not because of losing the weight and cutting her hair but because she was different she wasn't hiding behind a wall any longer. Angel would catch Meghan looking at her time and time again.

She again went home and went onto the computer in hopes that Meghan was on. She was and Angel left her a message, she tried to be blunt and told her how she felt. She told her that she thought they should go out at least once and try something different instead of going out in public with just men. Angel went and picked Meghan up and as Meghan walked towards the car wearing a Silky orange and black shirt unbuttoned with a white tank top on underneath. As she got into the car, Angel was overwhelmed by how good she smelled. Angel told herself before that night and before picking her up that she wasn't going to make it into any sort of romance or relationship, but she looked so good and smelled so good it made it hard for Angel. Angel planned on bringing her to a night club where she knew that the usual bunch would be there; this way she wouldn't feel anything towards Meghan right away.

Angel asked her if she would like to dance and she didn't refuse, but she did mention that she never dances in front of anyone. They moved closer and closer to one another and as their bodies moved to the music it was as if they danced together a hundred times. Angel had danced with woman before but this was different, if people were to watch them they would assume they had been in a relationship for years. Angel never flaunted her gayness in front of anyone before but with Meghan it wasn't flaunting it felt so natural. She didn't care who was watching or pointing at them she wanted to show everyone this beautiful woman who wanted her and loved dancing with her. After a couple of songs they went and sat down to get refreshment. As they started to talk it felt almost magnetic when their bodies began to get closer and their legs intertwined. It was as if Angel had no control over her functions and her hand grabbed Meghan's knee and then they kissed. It felt as though this was Angel's first kiss ever. She got goose bumps, her knees began to shake and there were chills going up her spine. Meghan spent the night at Angel's house and it just felt right as they woke up still touching.

That same morning Angel had to go to her mom's house to help her with something and Meghan asked if Angel didn't mind she would love to meet her mom. They kept there romance a secret for a little while after that first night. Angel had never felt this way before even with Chanel sometimes the physical didn't hold on to the emotional as it did with

Meghan. Angel just knew in her heart after that first kiss Meghan was the one.

She was now just worried about how the rest of the family would be, she had one cousin who was with the same woman for over ten years never did they hold hands, kiss or show affection in front of anyone. Everyone knew but just like everything else in their family they brushed it under the rug. Angel finally let everyone in on her little secret and after that her other cousin came out and admitted that she too was gay and has been in a relationship for over a year now.

Angel finally graduated Empire Beauty School at the highest level that anyone could achieve and with the most sales. Her life was finally making sense. Meghan and Angel finally told the family they were in fact dating. The children were still not letting Meghan in with open arms, but Angel knew that very seldom will kids approve of who their moms bring home she also knew that the kids would be happy as long as she now was happy.

Under circumstances that Meghan and Angel could only guess to be bias they were both let go from the job they both shared for three years at. Angel went to work as a Hairdresser in a great salon and Meghan graduated as an LNA and went to work for the local Hospital.

Lil divorced Jerry after his lies finally caught up to him and she is now married to a wonderful man that treats her like the queen she is.

Summer married an accountant and they have two wonderful children. A boy who is gorgeous and may in fact be the smartest kid alive. A little girl who is beautiful like Summer and her smile will take anyone bending to the ground at her feet.

Alex is about to be eighteen and he is a typical teenager finding trouble everywhere he goes. He acts like a tough guy but when you look into his eyes you can see into his soul and realize that he is gentle. Still Angels little sister and brother have their problems and wont let anyone in reach of their hearts.

Summer and Alex have been making it their mission to find the missing pieces in their lives. They had learned that over the years, Leon had many children and they have met a few of them and have brought Diamond on this quest with them. Angel is in hopes that someday they will feel complete as she does and realize they have all the family they need right around them.

Brad and Denise have been around more, Brad and Angel rekindled their relationship as father and daughter but more importantly as friends.

They talk on the phone at least once a week. Colby has two children a boy and a girl, both of which Angel hardly knows because her and her brothers relationship has never really taken off. They still get a gift for Christmas that say from Aunties Angel and Meghan. Katrina is still trying to find out that she truly is and Angel hopes one day that she can in fact be the big sister to them that she has always wanted to be.

Diamond has made Angel proud in every way a daughter could. She has looked into modeling and could be very successful at it but just isn't ready. She is learning how to drive. She writes beautiful poetry and draws sometimes. She works part time at a pizza place. She still sometimes will find her mom peaking in the window with those proud eyes. You can just look at Diamond and see that she is a hard worker and wont let anything stop her from getting what she wants. Angel knows that is a trait that she gets from her, and sometimes will get her into trouble just as it has done for Angel. Sometimes being like her mom gets her into fights with her dad because she is old enough to speak her mind, and that she does. Angel makes sure there isn't a day that goes by that she doesn't let Diamond know that she is proud of her and she loves her.

Dave is twelve and is content in being a preteen. He is a wonderful artist and will draw out his feelings. There are girls that call him everyday and God help everyone if he acts like his uncle Alex who has always carried on with more than two girls. He looks just like his dad and acts a lot like him and has tried more than once to tell his mom how it is, but she is making him into the man that a woman will be proud to have.

Dwayne still isn't the best father he could be, but hopefully someday he will come to his senses. Dwayne and Jasmine became married and Angel was at their wedding. Now Angel sees Jasmine in the same pain she had gone through for so many years. Sometimes Angel thinks Dwayne might even treat Jasmine worse than he ever treated her or she might just be in denial still. She watches on as their little boy cries for them t stop fighting in the same way their children begged.

Leon has been released and has lost all contact with his family. Diamond still fears that every now and then she senses someone watching her. Angel fears she might just be right.

As for Angel and her life she still has occasional nightmares and wakes up in a cold sweat picturing him on top of her. Sometimes she finds herself running to the kids rooms in the middle of the night holding her breathe just to hear the silence on the other side of the doors. Praying she doesn't hear Leon's moans while hurting her children and then being relieved just to find them sleeping. She is oddly satisfied to hear Diamond yelling at her and telling her to leave her alone and let her sleep or Dave kissing her goodnight all over again. She still can't walk through the woods without seeing Leon standing on top of her naked body. She's still not able to get up at night to go to the bathroom by herself Meghan walks with her every night. She still can't smell fresh paint or cut wood. She never goes into a garage and shuts the door behind her. She has never been able to make love to Meghan without a thought or two of Leon.

She never goes a day without looking into strangers little girl's eyes and wondering what pain she may going through at home. She never goes a day without thinking about Leon.

She asks herself will she ever forgive the people in her life that let this happen to her for so many years. The answer is yes, because God has given her the strength to forgive. She asks herself if his sentence was enough and she answers no because no matter how many years he spent behind bars it will never give her back the years that he had taken from her and continues to take.

As for Meghan and Angel they are still together and have been for years now.

As Meghan and Angel stand in front of a woman who is going to seal their future together. Angel notices a tear fall from Meghan's eye and a smile that could never be erased from her memory. They exchange their vows and know they are each other's forever. As they seal their marriage with a kiss Angel feels this rush come over her as the frightened little girl she once was disappears from her thoughts and clings to her heart because she is now and forever safe.

Please to everyone that has read my story, remember for everyday that you live in sorrow, pain or anger, you are taking away a day that could be filled with love and happiness. You are only as good as you make yourself, no one should be able to take that away from you. No one should be able to take your freedom, self worth, happiness or your body from you. Think of how many lives' you will change with the choice you make on this very day. What is life worth to you?

Angel Costello

Angel Costello received her Business Degree and Cosmetology License: she currently manages a Hair Salon. She volunteers as a Child Advocate in her spare time and is looking to help as many people out that are going through similar life styles as she has. She currently lives with her wife and children in New Hampshire and she leads a fulfilled life. She has had contact with Leon and his family.

CPSIA information can be obtained at www.ICGtesting.com
Printed in the USA
LVOW081646260412

279298LV00005B/189/P

9 781456 761868